WHOLE

BOWL FOOD FOR BALANCE

MELISSA DELPORT

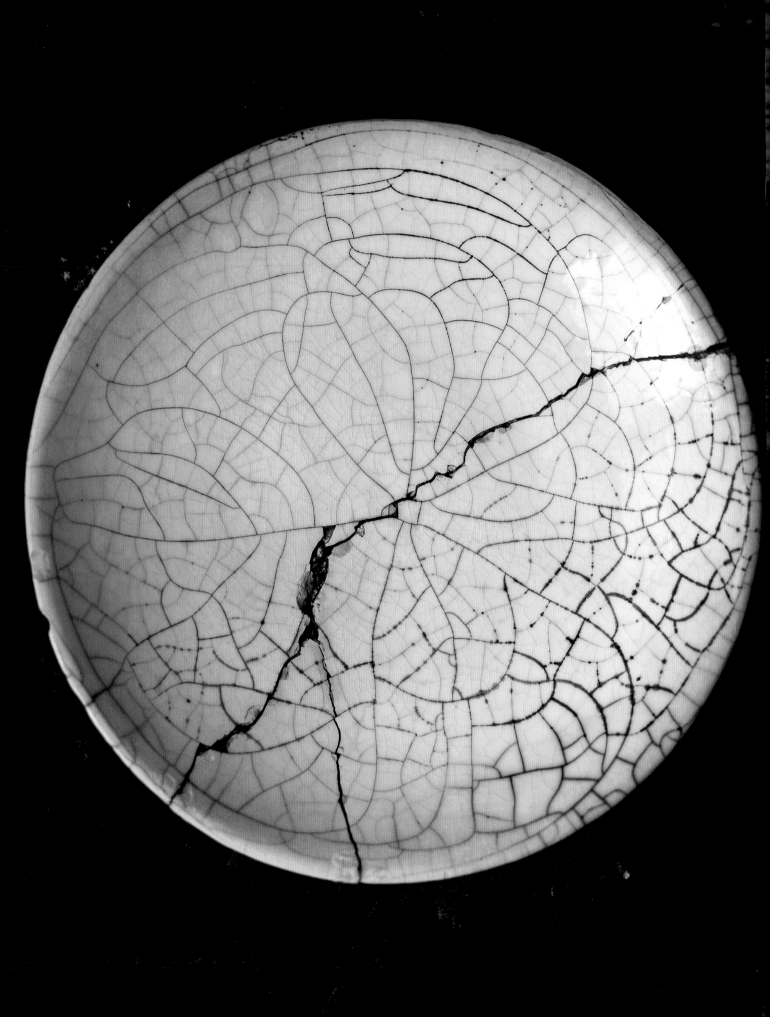

WHOLE

BOWL FOOD FOR BALANCE

MELISSA DELPORT

ACKNOWLEDGEMENTS

Creating this cookbook has been a dream come true and an incredible healing journey. Thank you to my partner Lauren. Your calm strength beside me on this journey has been invaluable. Thank you for reading and re-reading all I've had to say and for being the quiet to my storm. Thank you to my beautiful mother Sonja, who has been my biggest cheerleader, never faulting in your support and love. Thank you to my family for your unwavering love, testing recipes and allowing me to be the creative that I am today. Sarah, you were the silent grace that I needed when I realised that doing this single-handedly would be a very big mountain to climb – thank you for choosing to climb it with me. Tyla, thank you for being the ray of sunshine that you are and for working on this manuscript with me as if it was your baby too. Your meticulous proofreading was invaluable to me. Nikita, you are an angel sent to me – thank you for all the late-night conversations and moments of enlightenment, I am forever changed. Rose, with love and laughter you opened the door to a world of cooking that shifted me into the cook I am today, thank you. Last, but not least, thank you to my tribe for every single moment that you have cheered me on, tested recipes and shared your energy. You've pulled me out of doubt, showed me I can do it and walked this journey with me every step of the way. I love you all and I am eternally grateful.

Thank you to my wonderful publisher Linda for seeing a book from ten recipes and for choosing me. Thank you to Joy, my editor, for perfecting my words and helping me communicate my story and recipes. Thank you to my wonderful designer Helen for being the creative that you are, making me feel heard and helping me turn my vision into a reality. Having you as my team has been an experience I will never forget.

Published in 2018 by Struik Lifestyle
(an imprint of Penguin Random House (Pty) Ltd)
Company Reg. No. 1953/000441/07
The Estuaries, 4 Oxbow Crescent, Century Avenue, Century City, 7441
P O Box 1144, Cape Town 8000, South Africa

ISBN 978 1 43230 858 2

Publisher: Linda de Villiers
Managing editor: Cecilia Barfield
Editor and indexer: Joy Clack
Designer: Helen Henn
Photographer and food stylist: Melissa Delport
Photographer's assistant: Sarah Goodman
Ceramic bowls: Mervyn Gers Ceramics
Proofreader: Jennifer Leak

Reproduction by Hirt & Carter Cape (Pty) Ltd
Printed and bound in China

This book is printed on FSC®-certified paper. Forest Stewardship Council® (FSC®) is an independent, international, non-governmental organisation. Its aim is to support environmentally sustainable, socially and economically responsible global forest management.

CONTENTS

INTRODUCTION

MY FOOD PHILOSOPHY IS A SIMPLE ONE.
EAT REAL FOOD, MOSTLY PLANTS, BUT NOT TOO MUCH.

I discovered this way of eating from Michael Pollan, the American writer and journalist, and it has revolutionised my relationship with food and helped ease the overwhelming anxiety I used to feel around food and food choices.

Due to bad eating habits, and a general lack of 'fad diet' understanding at the time, I was put on my first diet at age 11. This set the tone for the next 15 years: pushing myself from one extreme to another with failed results amidst feelings of guilt and anger.

I was so busy listening to everyone else and every other diet book that I stopped listening to my body. I had lost the most valuable connection – the relationship with myself.

Becoming mindful of the food I eat, where it comes from and how it is prepared, coupled with my new-found food philosophy, has allowed me to move past feelings of futility and frustration and let love and nourishment flow in.

Any negative talk or anxious energy around eating is not healthy. And when you consider that most people eat three meals a day, or at least subscribe to the tenets of the contemporary diet – breakfast, lunch and supper – this harmful reinforcement can occur at every mealtime. However, this also gives you 1 095 opportunities every year to change that reinforcement to a positive one.

Our generation is lucky to have learnt the ugly truth about processed foods and the damage they do to our digestive systems and general health – cancer, hypertension, high blood pressure, diabetes. The reality is dire ...

All the dishes I have created and have chosen to share with you here are wholesome, healthy and delicious. I have avoided mass-produced, processed food in this book entirely.

Be present when creating your dishes. Take the time you deserve to create worthy fuel for your body. Savour each and every mouthful. It has made a world of difference in my life.

This book is centred around bowl eating and came about from Buddha bowls. What are they? Simply put, they are bowls of nourishment that contain healthy grains, raw or cooked vegetables, a healthy fat, a protein and a whole bunch of greens.

Eating from a bowl is comforting. The recipes in this book are all about home cooking and delicious flavours.

Conscious, considered consumption is the way forward and it is time for us to reclaim our health by making better choices.

I hope the recipes in this book will change something in you as they did in me. Healthy eating takes practice and time but it is singularly one of the most rewarding journeys I have ever undertaken. You'll have good days and bad days so it is important to remember that it's not about the destination of perfection, but rather a lifelong commitment to your health and wellbeing. Find what works, eat good food and love your body.

REACHING THE UMAMI

Discovered by the Japanese, umami is one of the five basic tastes, the others being sweet, sour, bitter and salty. The perfect description of umami is 'yummy'. In this book I cook with a lot of ingredients to create umami flavours.

My kitchen is always stocked with onions, garlic and organic tamari sauce. Why tamari? It is a gluten-free option to soy sauce and offers the perfect salt pop to any dish. When it comes to onions and garlic, they may be delicious but they don't agree with everybody. If you feel bloated or sluggish after eating them, rather listen to your body and skip the ingredients.

Take time when building and layering your bowls to create the ultimate umami moment when it's time to tuck in.

A NOTE ON BUYING ANY INGREDIENTS, AND THEIR LABELS

We have been so programmed to care about the amount of 'carbs' or 'calories' we consume that we don't read the ingredients on the back of labels. If you are eating maple syrup, then that should be the only ingredient.

Be aware of the amount of colourants and preservatives that are present in something you are considering buying. If you can't pronounce it then you shouldn't be eating it. On that note, real food doesn't come with a label.

LET'S TALK PANTRY

I want to share a little bit of information about the staples that I have in my kitchen at all times. These ingredients often form the base of my cooking and I consider them as my starting point. They will also help you with the recipes to come so I suggest having these ingredients stocked in your pantry.

Grains, beans and pulses are a neutral base upon which to build. Add freshness such as mint or ginger to brighten your bowls. Layer contrasts of cooking techniques, such as raw and cooked or roasted and blanched, to give your meal complexity in both texture and taste.

Whenever possible (and more often than not), I opt for organic ingredients.

I try to be a conscious consumer and know that I always have a choice when it comes to where I decide to spend my money. I like to think that in my own way, I'm making the world a little better.

Support local food markets and the farmers who grow the produce. Not only are you helping the little guy earn a living but you are also choosing a healthier option for your body and your family.

The reality is that we do not know how Genetically modified organism (GMO) and non free-range produce affects our bodies in the long run. Nourishing your body with real, fresh food is not only healthier and better for the environment, but it also tastes better.

Having a variety of cooking basics will allow you to develop flavours and cook with intuition, using your senses of taste and smell as your guide. Trust your palate. If something is too sweet, add a little salt. If something is too spicy (such as cayenne pepper), add a little sweetness (such as honey). Contrast your ingredients to build flavour.

Take the time to taste your food as you go about your cooking. So often I hear 'I don't have time to cook', but I want to encourage you to change that conversation with yourself because you deserve great tasting food that will nourish your body.

COCONUT OIL

I only cook with coconut oil and usually have a tub on the shelf ready to add a little to my dishes when needed. Remember, everything in moderation. I do not use excessive amounts of oil to cook, just enough to do the job.

OLIVE OIL

Used only for dressing salads or drizzled onto vegetables and soup. When you cook with olive oil you destroy the flavour as it has a lower smoke point than coconut oil. This means that at a certain stage the health benefits of the oil are lost. Rather save it for salads and enjoy the nourishing properties of the oil.

MAPLE SYRUP VS HONEY

The maple syrup I use in the book is 100 per cent maple. Not the refined type most commonly found in stores. I also source organic raw honey for my kitchen. Not only is it better for the environment, but the honey is sweeter. If you are vegan, using maple syrup, agave or coconut sugar is a great alternative to honey. I have learnt that there is always a great alternative option to an original ingredient when needed. Instead of sugar, try coconut sugar or instead of cow's milk, try coconut milk.

CITRUS

I always have an abundance of citrus in my kitchen, especially lemons, oranges and limes. Not only is it wonderful for gut health to have fresh lemon water every morning, but it can elevate a dish and make flavours pop. I use citrus in dressings and squeezed directly onto food. Zesting a lemon or lime adds an element of freshness to a dish.

HERBS AND SPICES

When it comes to herbs I like to keep things fresh, but using the dried version is also perfectly delicious. Keep a large variety of herbs at hand as they are behind the magic in dishes. If you have a sunny windowsill, why not try to grow some fresh herbs? You will have less food waste and it is so rewarding using food you have put love and energy into, plus you will know that it's truly organic! I grow basil, oregano, mint, chives and lemon thyme to name a few and use them liberally in my cooking.

Spices are one of the fundamentals of flavouring your food. I am all about slow cooking and have shared my labours of love in this book (although there are quick and easy recipes as well). Using the right combinations of spices can result in not only intensely beautiful flavours but also food that has great health properties.

Stock up on a variety of spices from turmeric, cayenne pepper, cardamom to cinnamon, all of which add a little flare in the kitchen. As you work your way through this book you will see that I use them often. Be inspired to adjust and play within the boundaries of the recipes. If I have a little heat but you would like more, why not try that?

SEEDS AND NUTS

I like to stock up on seeds and nuts and store them in jars to keep them fresh. They are so wonderful to add to almost every meal. If a salad needs a crunch or if you need a healthy snack, they will come to the rescue. Toast them or simply have them raw. Carry some around with you when you are on the run. They can keep blood sugar levels stable and are high in fibre. A great way to prevent a sugary binge at 4 pm.

VEGETABLES AND FRUIT

Vegetables are at the centre of my kitchen and the heroes of my dishes. I buy my produce from local organic markets as much as possible. Always wash vegetables and fruit to rid them of any traces of pesticides and chemicals.

When it comes to cooking vegetables you can blanch, roast, steam and sauté them or even have them raw. I like to keep my vegetables as fresh as possible and limit the cooking time unless I am roasting them or the recipe requires it. Lightly cooking vegetables helps the body to digest them while still keeping all their wonderful health properties intact. Buy the rainbow as much and as often as possible. Each and every colour of fruit and vegetable offers different vitamins, micronutrients and minerals.

Try to keep fruit separate to other meals as it allows the body to digest them better. Whether you are indulging in a fruit or making a smoothie bowl, mix it up and try a variety. Remember, everything in moderation.

GOING GREEN

It is surprisingly easy to eat your daily greens if you keep them readily at hand. You can add greens to smoothies (a wonderful alternative to eating a whole salad), a breakfast toast with boiled eggs, a salad bowl or fold them through a delicious soup or stew. Greens are very important in aiding digestion and can offer an array of flavours. Rocket gives a dish a pepper kick whilst butter lettuce offers a crunch of sweetness. The wonderful thing is, if you don't like a specific green there is a wide variety and you are bound to find a few you love! If watercress doesn't tickle your taste buds, why not try baby spinach? I try to incorporate a generous handful of greens into every meal. It is a healthy habit that will not only benefit your liver (dark leafy greens aid liver function), but also result in a happier, healthier you.

DAIRY AND EGGS

I have limited my use of dairy in this book. When you use dairy, try and source it from a local farmer. Mass-produced dairy is no longer healthy or ethical due to the growth hormones and antibiotics that are being administered to these animals. These chemicals can affect our health. Great substitutes that I use liberally in my kitchen are coconut milk and unsweetened almond milk.

If you don't like cow's milk, you can try goat's milk. If you would like to cut down on dairy, then leave it out altogether.

I only use free-range eggs from my local farmers' market.

MEAT

Save meat for special occasions and, where possible, make an effort to ensure that it is ethically sourced. The reality of feedlots and how animals are treated can no longer be ignored. Support a local butcher who sources free-range, organic meat rather than the supermarket.

It is okay to not eat meat everyday, at every meal. This book has limited meat recipes, but it is not a vegetarian cookbook. I want to show you how easy it is to eat less meat. Not only is it easier on your budget and the environment but it is healthier for your body to eat more vegetables. As for the protein you are worried about? Don't worry, all the meals have all the nourishment and protein your body requires. There are excellent plant-based proteins such as quinoa, lentils and beans. They form a great base to many dishes and are a wonderful substitute to meat.

GRAINS, LEGUMES AND PULSES

I keep jars full of gorgeous grains in my pantry. I love them! They are brimming with vitamins and minerals, not to mention that they are high in protein and fibre, and you can add a grain to most dishes and salads. I try to avoid anything processed or bleached and always opt for GMO free. When it comes to chickpeas and lentils, soaking them overnight is best and can aid digestion.

I try to avoid tinned food. Of course, the reality is that it isn't always possible to do so. We all lead busy lives and sometimes we forget to soak the chickpeas overnight. Try your best to replace tinned food with fresh food.

Tomato onion mix is as simple as chopping one onion and a few tomatoes. The flavour is better and there are less preservatives.

FOOD PREP

Cooking your food ahead of time is a wonderful way to avoid unhealthy eating as well as food waste.

Cook your grains, lentils and beans and store them in an airtight container in the fridge.

Roast your vegetables and do the same. I suggest you do two trays at a time. Make some hummus and keep it in the fridge for dipping, spreading or for adding a dollop to a salad. Keep fresh greens along with a variety of seeds and nuts.

This way you will always have food available when you are hungry and need to grab a meal on the go. Pick one night a week to be present in your kitchen and create the food you want to eat for the week to come. Always remember that you have the option to freeze your food and warm it up whenever you need it.

GRAINS AND LEGUMES

RICE

Rice has natural hydrating properties because of the amount of water it absorbs while cooking. It also balances blood sugar levels and helps control mood swings, which is why I dub it the happy grain.

Wild and brown rice can be used to fill up a fresh summer salad or as a base for any recipe. Make sure to avoid white rice as processing has stripped it of its nutritional value.

POPCORN

While popped corn doesn't have high levels of nutrients, it is very high in fibre and is a much healthier choice than many processed and store-bought snacks. This movie night favourite makes for a great snack on or off the couch, so get creative with herbs and spices or even try something a little sweeter.

QUINOA

With its soft nutty flavour, quinoa is one of the few plant sources that is a complete protein. This makes it a great substitute for meat, with all the amino acids you need and none of the drawbacks. Did I mention there are three colours from which to choose?

CHICKPEAS

Also known as garbanzo beans, chickpeas are high in calcium and magnesium, which help with maintaining optimal bone health. They are very versatile and used in many types of cuisine. You can eat them in salads, roasted as a snack, in stews, or with pretty much anything.

LENTILS

These little guys are very rich in vitamin B and are one of the best probiotic foods around. High in fibre, you can enjoy them in a salad or in a warm hearty stew. Red lentils are easiest to digest, so start with those if you've never tried lentils before. You will not be disappointed.

OATS

Oats are beneficial for managing stress and excellent for treating symptoms of fatigue and autoimmune diseases. They can also help you pack in energy for the day when you eat them for breakfast.

PEARL BARLEY

Aside from the many vitamins and minerals it contains, barley is great for lowering cholesterol due to the soluble fibre beta-glucan.

COOKING INSTRUCTIONS

Preparing grains and legumes is really simple once you know the basics. All you have to do is follow some basic rules. I like to use vegetable stock as the liquid in place of water as it will give the dish more flavour. If you are just using water with the grain, then make sure you season it with a pinch of salt. If you allow the grains to steam for another 10 minutes with the lid on and off the heat after cooking, it makes them fluffy and allows them to expand a bit further.

I've chosen the following grains and legumes based on their variety in taste and nutritional benefits. Here are my tips on how to make them perfect every time.

QUINOA

1 cup uncooked quinoa serves 4

The ratio: 1 cup quinoa to 2 cups boiling water

INSTRUCTIONS

Add the water and a pinch of salt to a saucepan and bring to a simmer over medium heat.

Add the quinoa and cover with a lid.

Simmer for 15 minutes.

Remove from the heat, keeping the lid on, and steam for another 10 minutes.

Fluff the quinoa using a fork and serve.

CHICKPEAS

1 cup uncooked dried chickpeas serves 2

The ratio: Enough water to cover the chickpeas

INSTRUCTIONS

Soak the chickpeas overnight.

Rinse the chickpeas and drain. Add them to a saucepan and cover them with water (about 1 cm above). If you want to spice things up, use vegetable stock in place of the water.

Cover with a lid and boil for 1½ hours or until tender.

Take them off the heat and drain.

When you're going through the effort of making chickpeas, I always feel it's better to make more than you need immediately as you can always save them for later. You can use them to make hummus, roast them or simply add them to a dish as is.

POPCORN

½ cup popcorn kernels serves 2

INSTRUCTIONS

Mix 2 teaspoons coconut oil and the popcorn in a medium saucepan over high heat and cover with a lid. Wait for the kernels to start popping and once they are halfway popped, lift the saucepan, holding the lid down, and quickly swirl it to help the remaining kernels get to the bottom so they can pop.

When you no longer hear popping, remove the saucepan from the heat and season with salt to taste.

LENTILS

1 cup uncooked dried lentils serves 4

The ratio: 1 cup lentils to 3 cups water

INSTRUCTIONS

Add the water to a saucepan and bring to a simmer over medium heat.

Add 1 sachet (if concentrate) or 1 teaspoon (if powder) vegetable stock.

Add the lentils and cover with a lid.

Simmer for 25 minutes.

Keep an eye on the lentils; if they get too dry you can top them up with more water.

Taste the lentils after 25 minutes.

Some people like lentils al dente while others like them softer. If the latter is the case then cook them for slightly longer.

They should be ready after 30 minutes.

WILD/BROWN RICE

1 cup uncooked rice serves 4

The ratio: 1 cup rice to 2½ cups water

INSTRUCTIONS

Add the water and a pinch of salt to a saucepan over medium heat and bring to a simmer.

Add the rice and simmer, uncovered, for 25 minutes.

Don't stir the rice during cooking or else you risk making it stodgy.

Taste the rice. If it is slightly al dente remove from the heat, keep covered and steam for another 10 minutes.

SUNRISE BOWLS

I am obsessed with breakfast. So much so, I wanted to create delicious, balanced bowls that will offer a little something for everyone. It is such a treat to be able to explore different food combinations that aren't your conventional fried eggs and bacon or a bowl of cereal.

Breakfast plays a vital role in keeping energy levels balanced throughout the day. Practise listening to your body and become mindful of the food that fuels you. Become aware of how you eat your breakfast. Get up a little earlier (even 15 minutes will give you ample time) to spend a moment on yourself before rushing out the door.

What keeps you satisfied? Is it fruit or something heartier? Eggs or oats?

I have learnt not to cut corners by fuelling up first thing with sugary pastries or processed cereals. It causes havoc with my blood sugar for the rest of the day.

This chapter shows you the wonderful dishes you can create that are packed with nutrients and are a unique take on a meal that is often eaten on the run.

Taking time on your breakfast is important because it sets you up for the day ahead. If you are short on time, try Pajama Oats (see page 21) or one of the smoothie bowls. Or have the family over for the Avo Hash bowl (see page 27).

SUNSHINE CHIA

MANGO AND CHIA PORRIDGE (VEGAN)

SERVES 2

Chia seeds are ancient seeds that date back to the Aztec era. They can be found at most health stores or in the health section at your local supermarket. You can add them to smoothies or sprinkle them over your oats.

½ CUP CHIA SEEDS

1 CUP ALMOND MILK

1 CUP COCONUT MILK

1 TABLESPOON PLANT-BASED
   PROTEIN POWDER

1 TEASPOON HONEY

½ CUP DICED FRESH MANGO

¼ CUP RAW COCONUT FLAKES

EDIBLE FLOWERS (OPTIONAL)

In a medium-sized frying pan over medium heat, add the chia seeds and almond milk and cook for about 10 minutes. The chia seeds will soak up the liquid. Slowly add the coconut milk to the mixture when it starts to look a little dry.

Add the protein powder and honey and mix well. Once all the liquid has been added and the consistency is like porridge, remove from the heat.

Add the chia seed porridge to the bowls and decorate with mango and the coconut flakes. If you find some edible flowers, use these to make the bowl beautiful. Beautiful food brings joy and joyous food is good energy!

HEALTH FACT

Chia is one of nature's richest antioxidants. It can prevent premature skin aging and is also very high in fibre, which promotes digestive health.

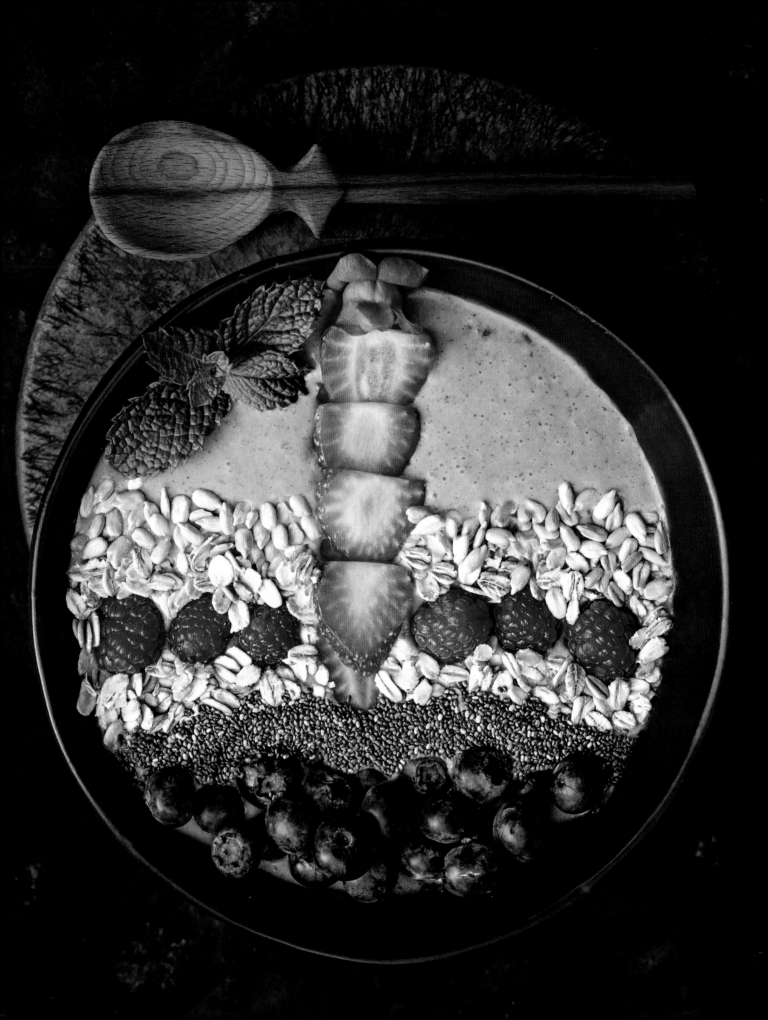

HAPPY HEART

STRAWBERRY AND ACAI SMOOTHIE BOWL (VEGAN)

SERVES 1

Smoothie bowls are a great way to have breakfast on the run. They can be prepared the night before or you can portion out your smoothie ingredients and freeze them, ready for the blender in the morning for a quick and healthy breakfast.

1 BANANA
1 CUP STRAWBERRIES
1 TABLESPOON CHIA SEEDS
½ CUP ALMOND MILK
⅓ CUP DESICCATED COCONUT
2 TABLESPOONS ACAI BERRY POWDER
3 BLOCKS ICE

This is a quick and easy one. Just blend all the ingredients together and decorate to your liking.

HEALTH FACT

Acai is a berry that you can buy in powder or liquid form. It has a beautiful deep purple colour. It is a superfood that has immune-boosting and anti-aging properties and is very high in antioxidants.

THE MEAN GREEN

AVOCADO, SPINACH AND BERRY SMOOTHIE BOWL (VEGAN)

SERVES 2

Don't be afraid of a green smoothie. Just because it's green, doesn't mean it isn't delicious.

SMOOTHIE

- ¼ RIPE AVOCADO
- 2 MEDIUM-SIZED RIPE BANANAS, SLICED AND FROZEN
- 1 CUP FRESH OR FROZEN RASPBERRIES
- 2 HANDFULS BABY SPINACH
- 1½ CUPS COCONUT WATER
- 1 TABLESPOON FLAXSEED MEAL
- 1 TABLESPOON MORINGA POWDER
- 2 TABLESPOONS ALMOND BUTTER
- SQUEEZE OF LEMON JUICE

TOPPINGS

- GRANOLA (SEE NUTTY CRUNCH, PAGE 22)
- CHIA SEEDS
- FRESH BERRIES
- COCONUT FLAKES
- HEMP SEEDS
- RAW OR ROASTED NUTS

Add all the smoothie ingredients to a blender and blend until smooth. Add the smoothie to a bowl and then decorate with toppings of your choice, making this bowl delicious for the eyes too. I've given a list of what I like to pair with mine.

HEALTH TIP

Adding greens such as baby spinach to a smoothie is a great way to pack in your vitamin K and green vegetables for the day, first thing in the morning.

PAJAMA OATS

OVERNIGHT OATS WITH BLUEBERRIES (VEGETARIAN)

SERVES 2

This is another great meal for people who have busy or stressful mornings and don't have time to make a wholesome breakfast to start the day off right. You can prepare overnight oats two days in advance. I like to put them in glass jars so they are ready to eat in the morning with no hassles or fuss.

1¾ CUPS KEFIR (OR YOGHURT SUBSTITUTE OF YOUR CHOICE)

¾ CUP ROLLED OATS

¼ CUP ALMOND MILK

¼ TEASPOON GROUND CINNAMON

1 VANILLA BEAN, SCORED LENGTHWAYS AND SEEDS REMOVED

2 TEASPOONS HONEY

½ CUP RAW ALMONDS

½ CUP COCONUT FLAKES

½ CUP FROZEN OR FRESH BLUEBERRIES

1 HANDFUL FRESH MINT LEAVES

2 TABLESPOONS CHIA SEEDS

Place the kefir, oats, almond milk, cinnamon, vanilla seeds and honey in a medium-sized airtight container and mix well. Cover with a lid and pop it in the fridge overnight.

To serve, add the almonds, coconut flakes, blueberries, mint and chia seeds. Pajama oats are great for when you're on the move and need to save some time in the morning. It's a good alternative to a quick breakfast such as cereal and will give you energy for the day ahead.

HEALTH FACT

Kefir is a powerhouse of goodness. Packed with probiotics, this fermented milk is good for healing inflammation of the gut and its overall health. It is also packed with calcium, aiding in the improvement of bone density.

NUTTY CRUNCH

PUMPKIN AND OAT HOMEMADE GRANOLA

SERVES 6

Not only can you use this for your breakfast in the morning, but it also serves as a sweet and crunchy snack that can satisfy your hunger and sugar cravings.

---

300 GRAMS PUMPKIN, PEELED AND DICED

3 CUPS ROLLED OATS

1 CUP RAW ALMONDS, ROUGHLY CHOPPED

½ CUP WALNUTS, ROUGHLY CHOPPED

½ CUP PUMPKIN SEEDS

⅓ CUP CHIA SEEDS

¼ CUP SUNFLOWER SEEDS

½ CUP RAW COCONUT FLAKES

⅓ CUP GOJI BERRIES

3 TABLESPOONS COCONUT SUGAR (OR
    SUGAR SUBSTITUTE)

½ TEASPOON SALT

1 TEASPOON GROUND CINNAMON

⅓ CUP COCONUT OIL

½ CUP MAPLE SYRUP OR HONEY

Preheat the oven to 180 °C. Line two 25 cm roasting trays with baking paper.

Steam the pumpkin for 15 minutes or until soft. Blend until smooth and then set aside in a bowl.

In a separate large mixing bowl, add the oats, almonds, walnuts, pumpkin seeds, chia seeds, sunflower seeds, coconut flakes, goji berries, coconut sugar, salt and cinnamon. Toss together and then set aside.

In a saucepan, add the coconut oil, maple syrup and the puréed pumpkin. Bring to a gentle simmer and mix well until combined. Add the wet mixture to the large mixing bowl of dry ingredients and mix well with a wooden spoon.

Halve the mixture between the two roasting trays and spread it into one even layer so it can bake evenly. Pop it into the oven and bake for 30 minutes, turning gently at the halfway point. This will break up the clusters, so you can decide how big you want them to be. Once the granola is golden brown, remove from the oven and allow it to cool completely.

You can store the granola in an airtight container and keep it for 10 days for breakfast time or just as a snack.

HEALTH FACT

Store-bought granola is generally very high in sugar. Making your own granola allows you to eliminate these unwanted sugars from your diet. Often things that appear healthy in the store, aren't, due to the processing these foods undergo and their hidden sugar content.

THE FEZ

TURKISH POACHED EGGS WITH SPICY SESAME DRIZZLE (VEGETARIAN)

SERVES 2

The Fez has everything that you want in a bowl: it has the crunch of the greens and seeds, the richness of the avocado and eggs, and the aromatic, herby yoghurt. You certainly won't be yearning for anything else after this breakfast. You can also prep the quinoa and the yoghurt dressing the night before to make this a reasonably fast breakfast.

1 CUP QUINOA

2 CUPS WATER

1 CUP PLAIN YOGHURT

1 HANDFUL FRESH PARSLEY, FINELY CHOPPED

1 HANDFUL FRESH DILL, FINELY CHOPPED

PINCH OF SALT AND PEPPER

JUICE OF 1 LEMON

4 EGGS, POACHED TO YOUR LIKING

2 GENEROUS HANDFULS BABY SPINACH

1 AVOCADO, SLICED

50 GRAMS GOAT'S CHEESE, CRUMBLED

1 TABLESPOON PUMPKIN SEEDS

SPICY SESAME DRIZZLE

1 TABLESPOON BUTTER

1 CLOVE GARLIC, CRUSHED

1 TEASPOON CHILLI FLAKES

½ TEASPOON CAYENNE PEPPER

1 TEASPOON SWEET PAPRIKA

1 TEASPOON SESAME SEEDS

In a medium-sized saucepan over medium heat, add the quinoa and water. Salt the water, cover and simmer for 15–20 minutes. Keeping the lid on, remove from the heat and steam for 10 minutes. Fluff the quinoa with a fork and set aside.

Meanwhile, place the yoghurt, parsley, dill, salt, pepper and lemon juice in a mixing bowl and whisk until combined. Set aside.

For the spicy sesame drizzle, add the butter, garlic, chilli flakes, cayenne, paprika and sesame seeds to a small frying pan over medium heat. Stir until melted, with the mixture well combined and starting to brown. Set aside.

Poach the eggs to your liking.

To assemble the breakfast bowls, layer the baby spinach, quinoa, yoghurt dressing, eggs, avocado, goat's cheese, pumpkin seeds and the spicy sesame drizzle. Season to taste.

FOOD TIP

Adding freshly chopped herbs and lemon juice to yoghurt not only makes a delicious dressing for this recipe, but for many salads as well.

AVO HASH

HASH BROWN BOWL (MEAT OR VEGETARIAN)

SERVES 4

For me, food is centred around love. To be able to share it with loved ones on a Sunday over a big fry-up, incorporating all the leftovers in the fridge, is what makes this recipe one of the best. Once a month I try to do a grocery sweep. This is where, for an entire week, I don't buy any groceries and I try to get creative with all the food in the fridge and pantry. It's truly amazing what you can create when left to your creativity and what is available to you in your kitchen. This hash brown bowl is one of those dishes where you can incorporate a variety of greens, meat and vegetables. All you need to do is fry them up individually and combine them at the end. I would save this recipe for the weekends. It is perfect for big family breakfasts and, of course, there is nothing wrong with a treat-yourself fry-up.

2 TABLESPOONS COCONUT OIL

4 LARGE POTATOES, CUBED INTO BITE-SIZED PIECES

SALT AND PEPPER

1 BROWN ONION, CHOPPED

1 CLOVE GARLIC, MINCED

4 SPRING ONIONS, CHOPPED

2 TOMATOES, CHOPPED

1 TEASPOON DRIED OREGANO

1 TEASPOON GROUND CUMIN

1–2 TEASPOONS CAYENNE PEPPER (OPTIONAL)

1 BUNCH KALE, STEMS REMOVED AND LEAVES TORN

1 PACKET BACON, DICED (OMIT TO MAKE THIS A VEGETARIAN MEAL)

80 GRAMS CHEDDAR CHEESE, GRATED

4 EGGS

2 AVOCADOS

1 LEMON

1 HANDFUL PEA SHOOTS

In a large frying pan over medium heat, add 1 tablespoon of the coconut oil. Add the potatoes and fry for 15 minutes or until golden brown and soft. Season to taste.

While the potatoes are cooking, add the remaining 1 tablespoon coconut oil, the brown onion, garlic, spring onions and tomatoes to a separate large frying pan over medium heat. Fry for 10 minutes or until soft. Add the oregano, cumin and cayenne pepper.

Once the potatoes are ready, add the kale. Stir until the kale begins to wilt. Don't overcook. Add the tomato and onion mix to the kale and potato mix. Mix well and season to taste.

If you wish, now is the time to add the bacon. Make sure to fry the bacon until it is nice and crispy and add it to the potato mix. Transfer to your serving bowls and top with the grated Cheddar cheese.

While the cheese is melting on the potato mix, fry the eggs to your liking in a separate frying pan.

Top each bowl with a fried egg and layer with freshly sliced avocado, a squeeze of lemon juice and a handful of pea shoots.

HEALTH FACT

Potato, the humble spud, is high in vitamins B and C, and iron. This is an energy-boosting food and great to eat as a snack when exercising. Potato is a good food, made unhealthy by the fact that it is mostly deep-fried.

THE SHROOM BOWL

MUSHROOM, CROUTONS AND POACHED EGG BOWL (VEGETARIAN)

SERVES 2

This is a decadent, creamy and crunchy breakfast. It is very satisfying while also packing in many healthy elements.
You can also try preparing eggs in different ways – scrambled, poached or boiled – to pair with this bowl.

2 TEASPOONS COCONUT OIL

1 RED ONION, CHOPPED

2 CLOVES GARLIC, MINCED

2–3 TEASPOONS FRESH ROSEMARY LEAVES

2–3 TEASPOONS FRESH THYME LEAVES

400 GRAMS MIXED MUSHROOMS

2 TABLESPOONS MASCARPONE

¼ CUP FINELY GRATED PARMESAN CHEESE

SALT AND PEPPER

2 EGGS

1 HANDFUL BABY SPINACH

CROUTONS (A FEW PER BOWL)

ZEST OF 1 LEMON

In a medium-sized frying pan over medium heat, add the coconut oil and onion and sauté until translucent. Add the garlic and herbs and fry for another 5 minutes. Remove the onion mixture from the pan and set aside in a bowl.

Turn the heat up to high and add the mushrooms, about a quarter at a time, frying for about 5 minutes with each addition. Adding them in batches prevents the mushrooms from boiling and allows them to fry, releasing their earthy flavours.

Once all the mushrooms are golden brown, return the onion mixture to the frying pan and turn the heat down to low. Add the mascarpone and Parmesan and fold through. Season to taste and remove from the heat.

For the eggs, cook them to your liking. Fried eggs work well with this recipe and add to the decadence of the creamy mushrooms. If you're wanting something less decadent, add poached or boiled eggs.

Build your bowl by layering your ingredients, starting with the spinach, then the mushrooms, eggs and croutons, and finish it off with fresh lemon zest.

HEALTH FACT

Eggs are a good source of vitamin B6, which helps maintain a healthy nervous system. They also help produce melatonin and serotonin, which are fundamental for sleeping patterns and mood stability.

FRESH BOWLS

It has been an amazing journey discovering how many delicious salads are possible, especially coming from a place where I believed the stock standard garden salad was the only option. You can add so much depth and dimension to a fresh bowl and there are always more combinations and flavours to explore. It's just about knowing what ingredients will balance and complement one another and, of course, it's all about experimenting.

Don't stop at ingredients; make sure you play around with different dressings and textures. A dressing can truly make a salad and it certainly doesn't have to be sweet and unhealthy to be good. Adding olive oil and lemon juice can lift the flavour profile of a salad and they're also good for you. Simply adding a tablespoon of apple cider vinegar can be enough as a dressing. Contrast cooked and roasted with fresh and crunchy.

Don't be tempted to turn to the safety of balsamic vinegar and feta to make a salad taste good. Turn to fresh ingredients and different combinations of flavour. You'll be surprised how easy it is to make a full and rewarding meal for your taste buds and your body. If you're interested, research which ingredients complement one another, and the multitude of health benefits each ingredient can offer.

Salads improve digestion and improve your mood. They are high in fibre, and they make you feel amazing. Nothing makes me feel better than a fresh bowl.

THE FIG AND GOAT

FIG AND GOAT'S CHEESE SALAD (VEGETARIAN)

SERVES 4

The fig really shines as the hero of this dish and is a prime example of how fruit can fit perfectly into a savoury dish.

2 RED ONIONS, QUARTERED

2–3 TEASPOONS FRESH THYME LEAVES

2 TEASPOONS COCONUT OIL

SALT AND PEPPER

3 TABLESPOONS OLIVE OIL

2 TABLESPOONS BALSAMIC VINEGAR

1 TEASPOON GROUND CINNAMON

10 RIPE FRESH FIGS, WASHED AND
    QUARTERED

2 HANDFULS ROCKET

50 GRAMS GOAT'S CHEESE, CRUMBLED

80 GRAMS HAZELNUTS, CRUSHED

Preheat the oven to 180 °C.

Add the onions, thyme, coconut oil, salt and pepper to a roasting tray and toss the ingredients until the onions are well coated. Roast for 25 minutes or until soft and some of the edges have started to char.

In a mixing bowl, add the olive oil, balsamic vinegar and cinnamon and mix well. Add the figs to the bowl and coat with the mixture.

Use a large bowl to assemble the salad. Layer the salad, starting with the rocket, then the red onions, figs and finally the goat's cheese. Top with crushed hazelnuts and serve.

HEALTH FACT

Figs are nature's detoxifier and goat's cheese is a great alternative to cow's milk cheese. See how you feel after you eat a certain type of food and pay attention to what works best for your body.

SALMON CRUNCH

SALMON AND EDAMAME GREEN BOWL

SERVES 1

This bowl illustrates how immensely satisfying a crunchy texture can be. When you pair crunch with healthy greens, it can be just as satisfying as a packet of crisps, but instead it rewards you and your body so much more.

---

1 TEASPOON BLACK SESAME SEEDS

150 GRAMS TENDER-STEM BROCCOLI, BLANCHED

250 GRAMS EDAMAME BEANS, SHELLED AND BLANCHED

4 SPRING ONIONS, FINELY CHOPPED

150 GRAMS SMOKED SALMON

1 HANDFUL SPROUTS

1 AVOCADO, SLICED

DRESSING

JUICE OF ½ LEMON

½ CHILLI, FINELY CHOPPED (OPTIONAL)

1 TABLESPOON TAMARI

1 TEASPOON HONEY

1 TABLESPOON OLIVE OIL

SALT AND PEPPER

Place the sesame seeds, broccoli, edamame, spring onions and salmon in a small salad bowl.

In a separate bowl, add all the ingredients for the dressing, mix well and season to taste. Pour over the salad and toss. Top with fresh sprouts and the avocado and serve!

This salad also goes wonderfully with brown rice. If you wish to use it, cook ½ cup as per packet instructions or refer to page 10, cool and add to the salad and dressing.

HEALTH FACT

Brown rice is an excellent source of magnesium. Along with the healthy fatty acids in the salmon, this is a bowl filled to the brim with goodness.

THE NIKITA

SERVES 2

This bowl was named after my friend Nikita because she has influenced me to adopt healthier habits. This bowl is a good example of how unique flavours and healthy ingredients can result in a delicious meal. Dubbed the Queen of Salads, Nikita showed me just how tasty healthy eating can be. Roasting the Brussels sprouts makes for an extra delicious flavour.

SALAD

- 200 GRAMS BRUSSELS SPROUTS
- COCONUT OIL
- SALT AND PEPPER
- 150 GRAMS TENDER-STEM BROCCOLI, BLANCHED
- 1 GENEROUS HANDFUL BUTTER LETTUCE
- 1 HANDFUL WATERCRESS
- 1 CUP BROWN RICE, COOKED PER PACKET INSTRUCTIONS
- 1 PEAR, CORED AND SLICED
- ½ CUP HAZELNUTS, CHOPPED

DRESSING

- 2 TEASPOONS CREAMED HORSERADISH
- 3 TABLESPOONS OLIVE OIL
- 1 TEASPOON HONEY
- JUICE OF ½ LEMON
- SALT AND PEPPER

Preheat the oven to 160 °C.

Place the Brussels sprouts on a baking tray with 2 teaspoons coconut oil and season to taste. Toss the tray to evenly coat the Brussels sprouts, and roast for 40 minutes or until slightly browned.

After blanching the broccoli, sauté it using 1 teaspoon coconut oil in a frying pan over medium heat. Sauté for about 2½ minutes for crunchy broccoli or longer if you like it soft.

In a small mixing bowl, combine all the ingredients for the dressing. Mix well and season to taste.

In a salad bowl, add the butter lettuce, either torn or whole to make little salad cups, and the watercress. Then add the Brussels sprouts, rice, broccoli and pear and pour the salad dressing over the top. Sprinkle the hazelnuts over for a bit of crunch and serve.

HEALTH FACT

Brussels sprouts are exceptionally high in vitamin K. Vitamin K sustains essential proteins, which protect your arteries and bones. It also helps fight cancer and diabetes.

FOUR GREENS SALAD

SPINACH, ROCKET, BROCCOLI AND SUGAR SNAP PEAS (VEGAN)

SERVES 4

I love making this salad when I'm craving something light, quick and fresh. It is a very simple salad, but sometimes that's all you want, a fresh and delicious bowl of greens. For a cheeky punch of flavour and colour, add roasted butternut.

SALAD

- 1 HANDFUL BABY SPINACH
- 1 HANDFUL ROCKET
- ½ CUP THINLY SLICED RED CABBAGE
- 1 AVOCADO, SLICED
- 250 GRAMS TENDER-STEM BROCCOLI, BLANCHED
- 1 HANDFUL SUGAR SNAPS PEAS, THINLY SLICED
- ¼ CUP PUMPKIN SEEDS
- SALT AND PEPPER

DRESSING

- 2 TABLESPOONS OLIVE OIL
- 1 TABLESPOON APPLE CIDER VINEGAR

Create a meal that is not only deliciously healthy, but also visually beautiful, by layering all the ingredients for this salad in a large salad bowl.

First, form a base with the spinach and rocket leaves. Then, stack the cabbage, avocado, broccoli and sugar snap peas. Top it off with a sprinkle of pumpkin seeds, dress the salad with olive oil and apple cider vinegar, and season to taste.

HEALTH FACT

Eating 1 cup raw broccoli is the vitamin C equivalent of eating one orange. Raw broccoli is delicious when dipped in homemade traditional hummus.

THE SALMON RUN

COURGETTE AND SALMON BOWL WITH BASIL AÏOLI

SERVES 2

This is the perfect brunch bowl and a bit of a 'show off' with the aïoli and salmon, but it is so quick and easy to make. Once you know how to make this basil aïoli, you can recreate it to add to a multitude of other dishes.

BASIL AÏOLI

2 EGG YOLKS

1 HANDFUL FRESH BASIL LEAVES

½–1 CLOVE GARLIC, CRUSHED

JUICE OF ¼ LEMON

5 TABLESPOONS OLIVE OIL

SALT

SALMON BOWL

1 CUP UNCOOKED BROWN RICE

2 TEASPOONS COCONUT OIL

280 GRAMS SALMON

SALT AND PEPPER

4 COURGETTES, SLICED INTO RIBBONS

½ CUP PEAS, BLANCHED

1 SMALL HANDFUL PEA SHOOTS

OLIVE OIL

JUICE OF 1 LEMON

1 EGG

For the aïoli, place the egg yolks, basil, garlic, lemon juice and olive oil in a food processor and blend until you reach a thick and creamy consistency. Add salt to taste and set aside.

Cook the brown rice as per the packet instructions or refer to page 10. Set aside.

In a large frying pan over medium to high heat, add the coconut oil and salmon and fry for 2–3 minutes on each side. Season the salmon and set aside.

In a large salad bowl, add the courgettes, peas, pea shoots and the brown rice. Add a good glug of olive oil and toss.

Shred the salmon using two forks. Add this to the salad and mix well. Add the lemon juice and season to taste. Fry or poach the egg, place on top of the salad and drizzle with basil aïoli.

HEALTH FACT

Salmon is high in omega-3 fatty acids, which help brain, eye and nerve development. Remember that sustainable sourcing is key.

ISLAND POKE BOWL

TUNA, AVOCADO AND EDAMAME POKE

SERVES 2

I hope that this poke bowl inspires you to develop your own poke bowl once you've learnt about the bowl basics. It has a healthy fat, a protein, a grain, greens, and a few different pops of flavour such as seaweed and mango. If you adopt these simple principles, the flavour combinations are endless.

1 CUP UNCOOKED BROWN RICE

200 GRAMS COOKED TUNA, CUT INTO
    1 CM CUBES

1 CUP EDAMAME BEANS, BLANCHED

1 MANGO, DICED

½ CUP SLICED ONIONS, FRIED UNTIL
    CRISPY

1 AVOCADO, SLICED

2 TABLESPOONS PICKLED GINGER

2½ TEASPOONS SESAME SEEDS

1 SHEET NORI SEAWEED, ROLLED AND
    SLICED

½ TEASPOON SESAME SEEDS

SALT AND PEPPER

DRESSING

2 TABLESPOONS TAMARI

½ RED CHILLI, FINELY CHOPPED

JUICE OF 1 LIME

1 TABLESPOON RICE WINE VINEGAR

Cook the brown rice as per packet instructions. If you want an extra magic touch to your rice, see page 10. Once ready, set aside.

In a small bowl, add all the ingredients for the dressing and mix well.

Now it's time to assemble the bowl. Don't be afraid to get creative with the way you build this bowl. Beautiful and unique presentation is a great way to connect with your food.

Once you have assembled the ingredients, drizzle over the dressing and sprinkle with sesame seeds. Season to taste and tuck in!

HEALTH TIP

Edamame beans are an excellent plant-based protein and are high in calcium and iron. Visit your local Asian supermarket if you can't find them at the grocery store. They add the perfect pop of colour and crunch to a meal.

FRILLS NO FUSS

KALE AND GRAPE QUINOA SALAD (VEGAN)

SERVES 6

I love this recipe because there is such a contrast of flavours, from the bitterness of the kale to the sweetness of the grapes.
If you couple kale with the right flavours then you will discover just how great its taste and texture is.

SALAD

250 GRAMS CHICKPEAS, COOKED

2 TEASPOONS COCONUT OIL

SALT

½ TEASPOON CAYENNE PEPPER

½ BUNCH KALE, STALKS REMOVED AND
    LEAVES TORN

2 TABLESPOONS OLIVE OIL

400 GRAMS SEEDLESS RED GRAPES,
    WASHED AND HALVED

½ SMALL RED ONION, FINELY CHOPPED

½ CUP FINELY CHOPPED RED CABBAGE

½ CUP WALNUTS

2 TABLESPOONS SUNFLOWER SEEDS

1 CUP QUINOA, COOKED AS PER PACKET
    INSTRUCTIONS

DRESSING

JUICE OF 1 LEMON

2 TABLESPOONS OLIVE OIL

2 TEASPOONS DIJON MUSTARD

1 TABLESPOON HONEY

2 CLOVES GARLIC, MINCED

SALT AND PEPPER

Preheat the oven to 180 °C.

Place the chickpeas on a roasting tray with the coconut oil, a good crack of salt and a light dusting of cayenne pepper. Roast for 25–30 minutes, giving them a toss at the halfway point. You want the chickpeas to be crunchy but not little rocks.

Add the kale to a large salad bowl. Drizzle with olive oil and gently massage the kale leaves until they wilt. Add the grapes, onion, cabbage, walnuts and sunflower seeds and toss together.

Mix all the dressing ingredients together in a small bowl and add to the salad bowl, along with the quinoa. Toss together.

Top with the roasted chickpeas just before serving. If you add them to the salad too soon they'll lose their crunch.

HEALTH FACT

Kale is very high in vitamins C and A, and iron, which gives your immune system the ammo it needs to keep you healthy.

AUTUMN JEWEL

TOMATO AND LENTIL SALAD (VEGETARIAN)

SERVES 6

This bowl is a very fresh tasting salad and each bite has crunch and a burst of sweetness from the tomatoes and pomegranate seeds. It's also a beautiful dish to brighten up your table.

SALAD

1 CUP BROWN LENTILS

3 CUPS VEGETABLE STOCK

200 GRAMS RED CHERRY TOMATOES, DICED

200 GRAMS YELLOW CHERRY TOMATOES, DICED

4 PLUM TOMATOES, DICED

300 GRAMS VINE TOMATOES, DICED

½ SMALL RED ONION, FINELY CHOPPED

1 RED PEPPER, DICED

1 HANDFUL KALE, STEMS REMOVED AND LEAVES TORN

1 POMEGRANATE, SEEDS REMOVED

1 HANDFUL FRESH OREGANO LEAVES

SALT AND PEPPER

DRESSING

2 CLOVES GARLIC, SLIGHTLY CRUSHED

½ RED CHILLI, FINELY CHOPPED (OPTIONAL)

½ TEASPOON GROUND ALLSPICE

1 TABLESPOON WHITE WINE VINEGAR

2 TABLESPOONS POMEGRANATE MOLASSES

1 TABLESPOON BALSAMIC VINEGAR

3 TABLESPOONS OLIVE OIL

1 TEASPOON HONEY

In a medium-sized saucepan over medium heat, mix the lentils and vegetable stock together. Cover and bring to a simmer and cook for 35–40 minutes. If the lentils dry out, top them up with water. You don't want the lentils to go soft and mushy, but you do want them to cook through, so don't be shy to taste test while cooking. Remove from the heat and let them cool for 10 minutes.

While the lentils cook, add all the tomatoes, the onion and the red pepper to a large salad bowl and mix well. Add the kale and toss.

In a separate small bowl, whisk all the dressing ingredients together until well combined. Remove the crushed garlic cloves and add the dressing to the salad.

Finally, mix through the pomegranate seeds, oregano and the lentils. Season to taste and enjoy!

FOOD NOTE

You can find pomegranate molasses at certain delis. Alternatively, you can make your own by reducing 4 cups fresh pomegranate juice with ½ cup brown sugar and ¼ cup freshly squeezed lemon juice until it is a syrupy consistency. It is important to note that blackstrap molasses, which is commonly found, is not an appropriate alternative for this dressing.

FOOD TIP

To remove pomegranate seeds easily, cut the pomegranate open, fill a bowl with water and start peeling the pomegranate under the water, separating the white and skin from the seed. This prevents the seeds from bursting and making a mess and they all sink to the bottom, making it easy to retrieve them and discard everything else.

HEALTH FACT

Lentils are a good source of dietary fibre.
They are high in iron, protein and vitamin B1.

SOUPS

One of my favourite things about soups (other than how delicious they are) is that none of your nutrients are lost. Instead of boiling vegetables and allowing the nutrients to leach into the water which is then thrown out, everything is contained in the pot. This is why soup is always great when you're sick, and also what makes it so tasty. Who doesn't crave a generous helping of chicken soup when they are feeling under the weather?

As a general rule, soups get better the longer you cook them – the flavours deepen and develop, leaving you with a fulfilling bowl of goodness. At the same time you can throw a delicious soup together relatively quickly.

Soups are a good option for food prep as you can freeze different portions and take them with you to work for lunch or reheat them for a quick dinner. And they're generally very easy to make.

Broths require much less cooking time and are ideal for a weekday cook where you are more pressed for time.

SPICY PRAWN SOUP

RED CURRY PRAWN SOUP

SERVES 6

This prawn soup is great for a dinner party. Why not play around with pairing it with one of the fresh or table bowls, such as the Island Poke Bowl (see page 43) or the Oh, Sweet Mustard (see page 148) to share with your friends?

RED CURRY PASTE

- 1 SHALLOT
- 1 STALK LEMONGRASS, CHOPPED
- 1–2 RED CHILLIES
- 2 CLOVES GARLIC, PEELED
- 2.5 CM PIECE FRESH GINGER
- 1 TEASPOON GROUND CUMIN
- ¾ TEASPOON GROUND CORIANDER
- 2 TABLESPOONS TOMATO PASTE
- 1½ TABLESPOONS FISH SAUCE OR
  SOY SAUCE
- 1 TEASPOON COCONUT SUGAR OR
  BROWN SUGAR
- 2 TABLESPOONS COCONUT MILK
- 1 TABLESPOON FRESHLY SQUEEZED
  LIME JUICE

SOUP

- 100 GRAMS FRESH OR FROZEN PRAWNS,
  SHELLED AND DEVEINED
- 1 PLUM TOMATO, CHOPPED
- ½ RED PEPPER, THINLY SLICED
- 1 STALK CELERY, FINELY SLICED
- 800 MILLILITRES COCONUT MILK
- 1 CUP WATER
- 1 HANDFUL PAK CHOI
- 1 TEASPOON COCONUT OIL
- 1 HANDFUL FRESH CORIANDER LEAVES
- 2 LIMES

Place all the ingredients for the curry paste into a food processor and blend until smooth. Set aside.

If using frozen prawns, place them in a bowl of warm water to thaw for 2 minutes. Remove the prawns from the water, place on a paper towel and pat dry. For fresh prawns, rinse, then place on a paper towel and pat dry.

To make the soup, add the red curry paste to a medium-sized saucepan over medium heat. Fry for 4–5 minutes to help release the flavour of the paste. Add the tomato, red pepper and celery and sauté for another 5 minutes.

Add the coconut milk and water to the saucepan, then add the pak choi and allow to simmer for another 5 minutes.

In a separate small frying pan over high heat, fry the prawns with the coconut oil for 2 minutes or until cooked through. Be careful not to overcook them. Remove from the heat.

Add the prawns to the soup and stir to combine. Serve hot with fresh coriander and a squeeze of lime.

OPTION

Serve with an egg noodle of your choice.

FOOD TIP

You can use the curry paste from this recipe as a base for any red curry you make. It's simply delicious!

ROASTED REDS

ROAST TOMATO AND RED PEPPER SOUP (VEGETARIAN)

SERVES 4

This recipe is all about the slow cook. The longer you roast the tomatoes, the sweeter they will become. This is a soup I would save for the weekends, but you don't have to miss out on it during the week. Freeze this soup in an airtight container and treat yourself to a slow-cooked meal fast on a regular week night.

SOUP

10 PLUM TOMATOES

3 RED ONIONS, HALVED

1–2 RED CHILLIES (AS PER HEAT
    PREFERENCE)

2 RED PEPPERS, SEEDED

2–3 TEASPOONS FRESH ROSEMARY LEAVES

2 TABLESPOONS COCONUT SUGAR

1 GARLIC BULB, LEFT WHOLE

COCONUT OIL

¼ CUP BALSAMIC VINEGAR

SALT AND PEPPER

2 CUPS VEGETABLE STOCK

BASIL PESTO

3 CUPS FRESH BASIL LEAVES

3 CLOVES GARLIC, PEELED

½ CUP FINELY GRATED PARMESAN CHEESE

JUICE OF ½ LEMON

¼ CUP OLIVE OIL

SALT AND PEPPER

TOASTIES

1 CIABATTA

250 GRAMS MOZZARELLA

BASIL PESTO (SEE ABOVE)

BUTTER

Place all the ingredients for the pesto into a food processor and blend until well combined. If the pesto is a little dry, add more olive oil. Set aside.

Preheat the oven to 180 °C.

Place the tomatoes, onions, chillies, red peppers, rosemary and sugar on a large roasting tray. Remove the excess skin from the garlic bulb and slice in half crossways. Open up the garlic bulb and place it on the roasting tray. (Note: Roasting the garlic bulb whole is easier than peeling each individual clove separately. Simply pop the cloves out of the bulb when done.)

Generously cover the ingredients with coconut oil, using your hands to ensure even coverage.

Generously drizzle the balsamic vinegar over the ingredients. Season to taste. Pop the tray in the oven and roast for 1 hour or until all the tomatoes are juicy and soft. Remove from the oven and keep the oven switched on for the toasties.

Transfer all the roasting tray ingredients, except for the garlic, into a large saucepan over medium heat. Pop the garlic cloves individually into the saucepan, discarding the skin. Make sure to use all the juices because that's where the flavour is. Using a stick blender, blend the soup until smooth. Add the vegetable stock and cover with a lid. Simmer for 40 minutes. Top up with water if it seems to be getting too dry or thick.

In the meantime, slice the ciabatta into 1-cm-thick slices. Make a mozzarella and basil pesto sandwich. Butter the outside of the sandwiches generously. Pop them into the oven for 5–10 minutes or until golden brown and toasted.

Serve the soup hot and the toasties fresh from the oven.

HEALTH FACT

Tomato is high in vitamin C and folic acid. The red pigment and antioxidant lycopene have been shown to lower and prevent the risk of breast, lung, skin, colon and prostate cancers.

SUN SPICE

SPICY BUTTERNUT SOUP (VEGAN)

SERVES 8

This is a classic crowd pleaser, so it's a great go-to recipe. Soup is a labour of love and is something you take your time to make. Put on some music and enjoy spending time in the kitchen.

---

3 TABLESPOONS COCONUT OIL

1 RED ONION, CHOPPED

2 CLOVES GARLIC, MINCED

1 TABLESPOON GRATED FRESH GINGER

1 RED CHILLI, CHOPPED (OPTIONAL)

2 TEASPOONS CAYENNE PEPPER
   (OPTIONAL)

1 CUP CHOPPED CELERY

1 LARGE CARROT, PEELED AND HALVED

1 SWEET POTATO, WASHED AND CHOPPED

500 GRAMS BUTTERNUT, PEELED AND
   DICED

4 CUPS VEGETABLE STOCK

¾ CUP COCONUT MILK

SALT AND PEPPER

CROUTONS (OPTIONAL)

1 HANDFUL FRESH CORIANDER

Add the coconut oil and onion to a large saucepan over medium heat and fry until translucent. Add the garlic, ginger, chilli and cayenne pepper. Keep stirring. Add the celery and stir until it starts to soften. Then add the carrot, sweet potato and butternut.

Once all the vegetables are mixed together, add the stock and top up with boiling water until the vegetables are covered. Simmer over medium heat for at least 1 hour. If you see the water level is low, top up with more stock or water. I let my soup cook for as long as possible, sometimes up to 2 hours. However, it can be served after 1 hour.

Once all the veggies are soft, blend the soup with a stick blender until smooth and thick. Simmer for another 20 minutes. Add the coconut milk and stir through. Season to taste.

Serve hot with croutons and chopped fresh coriander.

HEALTH FACT

Butternut is high in antioxidants, betacarotene, vitamins A, B-complex, C and E, as well as dietary fibre.

GET WELL SOUP

CHICKEN, TURMERIC AND GINGER SOUP

SERVES 2

When people talk about chicken soup for the soul, this is what they're talking about. It doesn't take too much effort or time, but has beautiful healing ingredients such as ginger and turmeric as well as some hearty, protein-filled chicken.

2 CHICKEN BREAST FILLETS
1 BROWN ONION, CHOPPED
2 CLOVES GARLIC, SLICED
1 TABLESPOON GRATED FRESH GINGER
4 BAY LEAVES
1 TABLESPOON TURMERIC
2 TEASPOONS CORIANDER SEEDS
SALT
4 CUPS VEGETABLE STOCK
2 TEASPOONS PEPPERCORNS
1 RED CHILLI, CHOPPED (OPTIONAL)
2 LARGE CARROTS, PEELED AND SLICED
200 GRAMS RICE NOODLES (OR NOODLE
    OF YOUR CHOICE)

In a medium-sized saucepan over medium heat, add the chicken, onion, garlic, ginger, bay leaves, turmeric, coriander, a sprinkle of salt, the vegetable stock, peppercorns and chilli. Add enough water to cover all the ingredients and bring to a boil. Reduce the heat and simmer gently for 12 minutes.

Remove the chicken from the pot and set aside to cool. Keep the stock simmering on the stove – if the water level gets a little low, top it up with hot water.

Using a fork, shred the chicken. Strain the soup, discarding the solids and keeping the broth. Return the broth to the stove. Add the carrots and shredded chicken and simmer for another 15 minutes or until the carrots are soft.

In the last 5 minutes of cooking, add the noodles to the broth and allow to cook.

HEALTH FACT

Ginger neutralises gastro-intestinal hormones, toxins and acids. It can soothe and treat stomach-related issues or flu symptoms.

GREEN SUPREME

SPINACH, COURGETTE AND COCONUT CURRY SOUP (VEGAN)

SERVES 4

Soups are a wonderful fridge clearer. When you have a lot of leftover vegetables, why not incorporate them into a soup?
It helps eliminate food waste and can result in a delicious meal.

---

2 TABLESPOONS COCONUT OIL

1 GREEN CHILLI, CHOPPED

1 TEASPOON CURRY POWDER

1 TEASPOON GROUND CUMIN

1 TEASPOON TURMERIC

1 LARGE LEEK, WASHED AND SLICED

2 SMALL SWEET POTATOES, PEELED AND
  DICED

2 LARGE OR 6 SMALL COURGETTES,
  CHOPPED

200 GRAMS FRESH SPINACH

80 GRAMS BROCCOLI

3 CUPS VEGETABLE STOCK

400 MILLILITRES COCONUT MILK

SALT AND PEPPER

OLIVE OIL

In a large saucepan over medium heat, add the coconut oil, chilli and spices. Fry for 1 minute until fragrant. Add the leek, sweet potatoes, courgettes, spinach, broccoli and the vegetable stock. Simmer for 20 minutes.

Blend the soup until smooth using a stick blender. Add the coconut milk and simmer for another 20 minutes. Season to taste and serve the soup hot with a drizzle of olive oil.

HEALTH FACT

Courgettes aid digestion because they are high in fibre.

WINTER SOUP

BEEF SHIN AND VEGETABLE SOUP

SERVES 4

When you're cooking red meat in a soup, don't rush it. The longer you cook it the more tender it will become. For soups, I always use meat on the bone because it creates a bone broth base that's packed with flavour, nutrients and minerals.

2 TEASPOONS COCONUT OIL

1 ONION, CHOPPED

2 CLOVES GARLIC, MINCED

600 GRAMS BEEF SHIN, WITH BONE

4 PLUM TOMATOES, CHOPPED

4 LARGE CARROTS, CHOPPED

1 CUP FINELY CHOPPED CELERY

1 CUP SHREDDED RED CABBAGE

3 LARGE LEEKS, WASHED AND SLICED

8 CUPS BEEF STOCK

400 GRAMS COOKED BUTTER BEANS

2 HANDFULS CHOPPED SPINACH

In a large saucepan over medium heat, add the coconut oil and onion and fry until translucent. Add the garlic and fry for another 5 minutes. Add the shin to the saucepan and fry until golden brown on all sides. Once the beef is golden brown, add the tomatoes, carrots, celery, cabbage and leeks. Add the beef stock and bring to a simmer.

Simmer for 1½ hours. If the water level gets low, top up with boiling water. Add the beans 20 minutes before the end of the cooking time. Once your soup is ready, fold in the fresh spinach and serve.

FOOD TIP

Fold through a generous handful of fresh baby spinach and chopped red cabbage 10 minutes before serving.

DOWN TO EARTH

ROASTED CELERIAC AND MUSHROOM SOUP (VEGETARIAN)

SERVES 6

---

*Celeriac isn't a common ingredient, but many local supermarkets stock it. Celeriac tastes like a combination
of turnip and celery so give it a try if you can find it. If you can't find celeriac then you can leave it out
of this recipe and simply create a beautiful mushroom soup.*

---

1 MEDIUM-SIZED CELERIAC (OPTIONAL)
COCONUT OIL
1 BROWN ONION, CHOPPED
2 CLOVES GARLIC, MINCED
2–3 TEASPOONS FRESH THYME LEAVES
300 GRAMS SHIITAKE (OR WILD)
    MUSHROOMS
1 POTATO, WASHED AND CUBED
1 SMALL SWEET POTATO, WASHED AND
    CUBED
4 CUPS VEGETABLE STOCK
¾ CUP COCONUT MILK
SALT AND PEPPER
2 TABLESPOONS TRUFFLE OIL
PARMESAN SHAVINGS

Preheat the oven to 180 °C. Lightly coat the celeriac in coconut oil and roast for 1 hour.

Meanwhile, in a large soup pot over low heat, add 1 tablespoon coconut oil and the onion. Fry until translucent. Add the garlic and thyme and fry for another minute. Add the mushrooms, a handful at a time, allowing each handful to heat up and fry. This will stop them from boiling and let them release their earthy flavour.

Add the potato and sweet potato cubes and top up with the vegetable stock. Bring to a simmer with the lid on. If the water level gets too low, you can top it up with water.

Once the celeriac is soft when pierced with a fork, remove it from the oven. Allow to cool for a few minutes and then peel. Cube the celeriac into bite-sized pieces and add it to the soup. Simmer for another hour. Once ready, add the coconut milk and stir. Season to taste. You can either serve the soup chunky or blend it with a stick blender.

Top with the truffle oil and Parmesan shavings and serve.

HEALTH FACT

Mushrooms are high in selenium and are the
only fruit or vegetable source of vitamin D.

OCEAN BOWL

MISO AND CLAM SOUP

SERVES 2

Clams are usually found in the frozen goods section of your local supermarket, while tofu and miso paste are readily available in Asian food stores. Tofu is a soya-based protein – in this recipe I cut it into cubes and add it to the broth, but you can also slice it up and fry it to top a bowl of noodles or a dish of your choosing. The wonderful thing about this soup is that it only takes 15 minutes to make.

6 CUPS WATER

100 GRAMS TOFU, CUBED

80 GRAMS SHIMEJI MUSHROOMS

500 GRAMS WHITE CLAMS

200 GRAMS RICE NOODLES

3 TABLESPOONS MISO PASTE (RED OR WHITE)

1 HANDFUL SPRING ONIONS, CHOPPED

TAMARI

In a large saucepan, bring the water to a boil. Add the tofu and mushrooms and cook for 2–3 minutes. Add the clams and cook for 2 minutes or until they pop open.

Meanwhile, cook the noodles as per packet instructions. Once the clams are ready, turn off the heat. When the liquid stops boiling, stir in the miso paste and then the cooked noodles. Top the soup with spring onions and a drizzle of tamari and serve.

HEALTH TIP

Miso is a fermented food and a great way to healthily flavour soups and broths. Mix in after cooking to maintain the live properties.

LIQUID GOLD

SAFFRON AND PUMPKIN SOUP (VEGAN)

SERVES 6

Saffron is the stigma of the crocus flower and is commonly found in the spices section of your local supermarket. It is native to Southwest Asia and the most costly spice by weight, and thus considered the gold of spices. Not only can it add a beautiful fragrance to a dish, but it has a pigment which imparts a rich golden-yellow colour to dishes.

1 PINCH SAFFRON THREADS
2 TEASPOONS COCONUT OIL
1 TEASPOON CAYENNE PEPPER
1 TEASPOON GROUND CUMIN
1 TEASPOON SMOKED PAPRIKA
1 TEASPOON GROUND GINGER
1 TEASPOON TURMERIC
5 BAY LEAVES
2 PINCHES SALT
4 CLOVES GARLIC, MINCED
4 MEDIUM-SIZED LEEKS, CHOPPED
400 GRAMS PUMPKIN, PEELED AND
   CHOPPED
4 LARGE CARROTS, CHOPPED
1½ CUPS RED SPLIT LENTILS
4 CUPS VEGETABLE STOCK
400 MILLILITRES COCONUT MILK
FRESH CORIANDER LEAVES FOR
   GARNISHING
OLIVE OIL FOR DRIZZLING
FRESHLY GROUND BLACK PEPPER

Add the saffron to a small cup of warm water and let it steep for 10 minutes.

In a large saucepan over medium heat, add the coconut oil and spices and fry for 5 minutes. Add the garlic and fry for 1 minute. Add the leeks, pumpkin and carrots to the saucepan and sauté, stirring often. When the vegetables have softened after about 5 minutes, add the lentils and fry for another minute. Add the vegetable stock and saffron water and simmer for 35–40 minutes. If the liquid runs low, top it up with extra boiling water.

Once ready, blend the soup with a stick blender until smooth. Add the coconut milk and stir through. Garnish with coriander leaves and add a drizzle of olive oil and a grinding of black pepper.

HEALTH FACT

Saffron alleviates symptoms of PMS. It also has cancer-fighting properties and can boost cardiovascular health.

ANCIENT GRAIN BOWLS

The Aztecs and Incas believed that amaranth and quinoa were foods of the gods and were highly praised. These grains, along with barley, millet, spelt, buckwheat and freekah, amongst others, have been around for thousands of years and have remained mostly unchanged, therefore giving them the title of ancient grains.

Many grains are gluten free and extremely versatile. You can play around with the combination of grains in all the grain bowls that are paired with various ingredients in this chapter to create meals that are not only tasty, but comforting too. Quinoa, buckwheat, millet and amaranth are all gluten-free grain options, whilst spelt is wheat-based.

Grains are also a great alternative to meat if you prefer a vegetarian or vegan option as they are high in protein and fibre. They are also high in omega-3 fatty acids and antioxidants so are good for your immune system and heart health.

I've only used a handful of ancient grains in these recipes, but you can interchange quinoa with spelt, or rice with freekah and play around with the combinations until you find what works best for you.

Grains form a neutral base to almost anything. You can use them in a breakfast porridge, in a savoury salad, or even as the hero in a dessert.

GROUNDED

ROASTED ROOT VEGETABLE BOWL (VEGAN)

SERVES 4

I'm a huge fan of root vegetables such as beetroot and sweet potato because you can make them delicious with very little effort. Simply pop them in the oven with a light coating of coconut oil and roast them until tender. They can be the hero of the dish or the perfect accompaniment to any creation.

---

6 BABY BEETROOTS, UNPEELED AND
    QUARTERED
1 HANDFUL BABY CARROTS, WASHED AND
    HALVED
2 RED ONIONS, QUARTERED
2 MEDIUM-SIZED SWEET POTATOES,
    SLICED INTO DISCS
1 SMALL BUTTERNUT, SLICED INTO DISCS
    AND SEEDS REMOVED
COCONUT OIL
2–3 TEASPOONS FRESH THYME LEAVES
SALT AND PEPPER
1 CUP UNCOOKED BROWN RICE
2 SWEET CORN COBS
2 GENEROUS HANDFULS BABY SPINACH
30 GRAMS PINE NUTS
OLIVE OIL
BALSAMIC VINEGAR
JUICE OF 1 LEMON

Preheat the oven to 180 °C.

Place the beetroots, carrots, red onions, sweet potatoes, and butternut on a roasting tray. Mix in 1 tablespoon coconut oil and the thyme and season to taste. Toss together until all the vegetables are evenly coated.

Pop the tray into the oven for 45–55 minutes, tossing halfway. I like my vegetables to have deliciously crunchy corners, but if you would like to roast them for longer it won't do any harm.

Cook the rice as per packet instructions or refer to page 10.

While the rice is cooking, ready a grill pan for the sweet corn. Lightly brush with coconut oil and grill until charred, turning regularly. If you do not have a grill pan, you can steam or boil the corn.

Now to assemble the bowl. Add the cooked rice and roasted vegetables to a large salad bowl. Slice the corn from the cob and add to the bowl. Top with the spinach and pine nuts. Drizzle with a good glug of olive oil, balsamic vinegar and the lemon juice. Toss well and season to taste.

HEALTH TIP

Root vegetables are very grounding foods. When you are feeling a bit spacy or stressed, these are the guys to turn to. They have mood-enhancing qualities and are very satisfying.

EARTH CHILD

ROASTED CAULIFLOWER, MUSHROOM AND COURGETTES (VEGETARIAN)

SERVES 4

This bowl is filled to the brim with beautiful, earthy flavours. I absolutely love truffle oil and believe that mushrooms are the diamonds of the kitchen, which is how the name of my blog, The Truffle Journal, came about.

1 HEAD CAULIFLOWER, BROKEN INTO FLORETS
5 SMALL COURGETTES, CHOPPED
300 GRAMS MIXED MUSHROOMS, CLEANED AND HALVED
2–3 TEASPOONS FRESH THYME LEAVES
1 TABLESPOON COCONUT OIL
SALT AND PEPPER
1 CUP UNCOOKED RED QUINOA
2 HANDFULS BABY SPINACH
40 GRAMS GOAT'S CHEESE, CRUMBLED
½ CUP WALNUTS, TOASTED AND CHOPPED
OLIVE OIL
TRUFFLE OIL

Preheat the oven to 180 °C.

Place the cauliflower, courgettes and mushrooms on a large roasting tray. Don't cut the mushrooms too small as they will get lost among the other vegetables and lose flavour. Mix in the thyme and coconut oil and season to taste. Toss all the ingredients and pop into the oven for 40 minutes.

Cook the quinoa as per packet instructions or refer to page 10.

Remove the vegetables from the oven. Add to a large salad bowl along with the cooked quinoa, baby spinach, goat's cheese and walnuts. Dress with a good glug of olive oil and toss together. Drizzle with truffle oil, season to taste and serve.

FOOD TIP

Did you know that you shouldn't wash mushrooms? They are like sponges and absorb water, so when boiled will become soggy. If you wipe or brush your mushrooms their earthy flavours will remain and shine through.

HEALTH TIP

Walnuts are a true brain food. They help improve your mood as their omega-3 content is the highest of any nut.

THE MOSAIC

POMEGRANATE AND AUBERGINE SALAD (VEGETARIAN)

SERVES 3-4

I hope this salad encourages you to explore the possibilities of tahini, the ground sesame paste found in the health section of most supermarkets. Tahini complements this dish beautifully and is an ingredient you should experiment with because of its versatility. It makes a hummus, it completes a dressing or can be used alone as a dressing.

SALAD

1 CUP UNCOOKED QUINOA
2 MEDIUM-SIZED AUBERGINES
1 TABLESPOON COCONUT OIL
SALT AND PEPPER
1 GENEROUS HANDFUL FRESH ROCKET
80 GRAMS POMEGRANATE SEEDS
50 GRAMS PINE NUTS, TOASTED

DRESSING

3 TABLESPOONS OLIVE OIL
2 TABLESPOONS GREEK YOGHURT
1 TABLESPOON TAHINI
JUICE OF ½ LEMON
SALT AND PEPPER

Preheat the oven to 180 °C.

Cook the quinoa as per packet instructions or refer to page 10. Once ready, set aside.

Cut the aubergines in half and then in half again, making wedges. Place them on a roasting tray and lightly cover with the coconut oil. Season to taste. Roast in the oven for 35–40 minutes or until golden brown.

In a small bowl, combine all the ingredients for the dressing and mix well.

In a large salad bowl, add the rocket and the quinoa and toss together. Add a generous dollop of dressing in the middle of the salad and place the aubergine wedges on top of the dressing. Save some dressing for the top. You can get creative here with how you arrange your wedges. Sprinkle with the pomegranate seeds and pine nuts. Pour a little more dressing over the top and serve.

HEALTH TIP

Aubergines are high in protein and the purple skin provides powerful antioxidants that protect your brain, lower cholesterol and move excess iron out of the body. Keep in mind that aubergines form part of the nightshade family. They don't agree with everyone, so explore to see if they work for your body.

FIREBIRD

CHICKEN FAJITA BOWL (MEAT OR VEGETARIAN OR VEGAN)

SERVES 2

This bowl is a good example of how meat isn't always the keystone of a meal. If you choose to leave out the chicken, you are left with a full and incredible vegetarian meal. If you would like to take it a step further and make this a vegan dish, then leave out the chicken and replace the yoghurt dressing with a squeeze of lemon juice and a glug of olive oil.

1 CUP UNCOOKED WILD RICE

2 CHICKEN BREAST FILLETS, SLICED 1 CM
   THICK (OPTIONAL)

1 ONION, ROUGHLY CHOPPED

1 RED PEPPER, SLICED

1 YELLOW PEPPER, SLICED

2 TOMATOES, ROUGHLY CHOPPED

1 TEASPOON GROUND CUMIN

1 TEASPOON CAYENNE PEPPER

1 TEASPOON GROUND CORIANDER

1 TEASPOON SMOKED PAPRIKA

2 TABLESPOONS COCONUT OIL

2 GENEROUS HANDFULS BABY SPINACH

200 GRAMS RED KIDNEY BEANS, COOKED

½ CUP SHREDDED RED CABBAGE

1 AVOCADO, SLICED

2 HANDFULS FRESH CORIANDER LEAVES

2 LIMES, QUARTERED

SALT AND PEPPER

SRIRACHA SAUCE (OPTIONAL)

DRESSING

2 TABLESPOONS FULL-FAT PLAIN YOGHURT

JUICE OF ½ LIME

1 TEASPOON FINELY CHOPPED FRESH
   CORIANDER

SALT AND PEPPER

Preheat the oven to 200 °C.

Cook the rice as per packet instructions or refer to page 10.

Place the chicken, onion, peppers and tomatoes along with the cumin, cayenne pepper, ground coriander, paprika and coconut oil on a roasting tray and roast for 25 minutes or until the chicken is cooked through. Make sure you spread the ingredients evenly so they all feel the heat. Once ready, switch the oven on grill for 5 minutes to add a little crisp. Remove from the oven.

Prepare the dressing by mixing all the ingredients together.

It is time to assemble your bowl. Take this moment to connect with your food and create something beautiful. You can start by layering the spinach and the rice. Remove the chicken from the tray and shred it using two forks, then add it to the bowl along with the vegetables. Add the kidney beans and red cabbage. Finish off with the avocado, coriander and a squeeze of lime. Season to taste and, if you want some heat, add some sriracha sauce. Serve with the dressing on the side.

HEALTH FACT

Coriander is one of the best treatments for removing heavy metals from the body. Use the seeds to combat digestive issues.

KOREAN KIMCHI

KOREAN BEEF AND SWEET POTATO

SERVES 4

Kimchi is a fermented food so don't cook it on a high heat for a long period of time as it will kill the probiotic properties. Kimchi can be found at your local healthstore or can very easily be made from scratch at home. Do some research on its health benefits and see if it works for your body.

400 GRAMS SWEET POTATO
COCONUT OIL
SALT AND PEPPER
TAMARI
HONEY
SESAME OIL
½ BUNCH KALE, STEMS REMOVED AND
    LEAVES TORN
2 CLOVES GARLIC, MINCED
1 CUP UNCOOKED BROWN RICE
300 GRAMS BRUSSELS SPROUTS, HALVED
80 GRAMS KIMCHI, CHOPPED
1 SHALLOT, DICED
400 GRAMS BEEF MINCE
TOASTED SESAME SEEDS

Preheat the oven to 200 °C.

Slice the sweet potato into 1-cm-thick discs. Place the discs on a large roasting tray with 1 tablespoon coconut oil. Toss so that the discs are evenly coated, season to taste and pop into the oven for 45 minutes, turning at the halfway mark. When ready, remove from the oven and set aside.

In a large bowl, mix together 2 teaspoons tamari, 2 teaspoons honey and 1 teaspoon sesame oil. You will use more of these ingredients a bit later. Add the kale to the bowl and massage the leaves until tender and coated.

In a separate bowl, combine 1 teaspoon sesame oil, the garlic, ¼ cup tamari and 2 tablespoons honey. Set aside.

Cook the brown rice as per packet instructions or refer to page 10.

Add 1 teaspoon coconut oil to a frying pan over low to medium heat. Add the Brussels sprouts and fry for about 10 minutes until golden brown, stirring often. Drizzle a third of the tamari and garlic dressing onto the Brussels sprouts, gently toss and transfer to the large salad bowl with the kale.

In the same frying pan, add half the kimchi and 1 teaspoon coconut oil and fry for 1 minute over medium heat. Once the rice is ready, toss it together with the kimchi and add to the large salad bowl.

In a medium-sized saucepan over medium heat, add 1 teaspoon sesame oil and 1 teaspoon coconut oil. Add the shallot and cook for 2 minutes. Add the mince and cook further, breaking it up with a wooden spoon until golden brown, or for about 5 minutes. Add the remaining tamari and garlic mixture and the other half of the kimchi to the mince and cook for 5 minutes, stirring often.

Once the mince is ready, add to the large salad bowl and top with the sweet potato. Sprinkle with sesame seeds, season to taste and dig in.

HEALTH FACT

Kimchi is loaded with vitamins A, B and C, but the biggest benefit is the healthy bacteria found in this fermented food that promotes gut health. It aids the intestines and stimulates better assimilation of nutrients in the body.

FRIDA'S FIESTA

MEXICAN REFRIED BEAN BOWL (VEGETARIAN OR VEGAN)

SERVES 4

This recipe is one of those where more is more. It's a family-style Mexican feast. You can add extra sides and build on to the recipe below. I have made this recipe using quinoa, but you can use brown or wild rice and turn it into a build-a-burrito affair or a taco Tuesday. This recipe is vegetarian, and if you leave out the sour cream it becomes vegan. Don't let that scare you because it is so tasty that it will satisfy even the fiercest meat eaters. Visit my Hola Guac (see page 136) and grilled Aztec Gold (see page 139) recipes in the Table Bowls section as possible add-ons to this feast.

1 CUP UNCOOKED QUINOA

½ RED ONION, DICED

COCONUT OIL

280 GRAMS DRIED PINTO BEANS, SOAKED
   OVERNIGHT

280 GRAMS DRIED RED KIDNEY BEANS,
   SOAKED OVERNIGHT

1 TEASPOON GARLIC POWDER

1 TEASPOON GROUND CUMIN

1 CUP VEGETABLE STOCK

SALT AND PEPPER

1 RED PEPPER, SLICED

CAYENNE PEPPER

1 HANDFUL BABY SPINACH

1 CUP SOUR CREAM (OPTIONAL)

Cook the quinoa as per packet instructions, leaving it to steam with the lid on and the heat off for the last 10 minutes of cooking.

Meanwhile, in a medium-sized frying pan over medium heat, add the red onion and 1 teaspoon of coconut oil and fry for 5 minutes, stirring often. Add the beans, garlic and cumin. Add the vegetable stock and cook for 5 minutes. Once cooked, use the back of a wooden spoon to mash the beans, allowing them to cook further into a paste. If the beans dry out while cooking, add a dash of water. Season to taste.

In a separate frying pan over high heat, add the red pepper, 1 teaspoon coconut oil and season with cayenne pepper to your taste. Fry for 4 minutes, until the peppers just begin to wilt, as you want them to keep a bit of crunch. Once ready, set aside.

It's now time to assemble your bowl, starting with quinoa as the base, then adding the bean mixture, red pepper and fresh baby spinach. Add the sour cream last, or serve it separately.

HEALTH FACT

Kidney beans are high in protein and fibre. They are a great source of a multitude of vitamins and minerals, including iron, magnesium and calcium.

BAKED TERIYAKI

CHICKEN OR TOFU TERIYAKI WITH PINEAPPLE (MEAT OR VEGETARIAN)

SERVES 5

You can replace the chicken in this recipe with tofu if you would like a vegetarian option.
Treat and cook the tofu exactly as you would the chicken.

1 CUP UNCOOKED WILD RICE

4 SKINLESS CHICKEN BREAST FILLETS,
    QUARTERED OR 400 GRAMS TOFU,
    SLICED

1 TABLESPOON COCONUT OIL

SALT AND PEPPER

150 GRAMS TENDER-STEM BROCCOLI

3 LARGE CARROTS, SLICED

½ CUP EDAMAME BEANS

½ CUP ROUGHLY CHOPPED PINEAPPLE

¼ TEASPOON SESAME OIL

2 MEDIUM-SIZED SPRING ONIONS, SLICED

2 TABLESPOONS SESAME SEEDS

TERIYAKI SAUCE

¼ CUP ORGANIC TAMARI OR
    DARK SOY SAUCE

5 TABLESPOONS HONEY

¼ CUP RICE WINE VINEGAR

1½ TEASPOONS SESAME OIL

3 CLOVES GARLIC, MINCED

1 TEASPOON GRATED FRESH GINGER OR
    GROUND GINGER

½ RED CHILLI (OPTIONAL)

½ TABLESPOON FLAXSEED POWDER

¼ CUP WATER

HEALTH TIP

Flaxseeds and ground flaxseed boost
energy, regulate oestrogen absorption and
aid digestion. They are a good source of
minerals, such as manganese (important for a
healthy brain and nervous system). Flaxseed
is a great replacement for cornstarch as
a thickening agent, and can be added to
smoothies for your daily fibre intake.

Preheat the oven to 200 °C.

Cook the wild rice as per packet instructions or refer to page 10.

In a medium-sized saucepan over medium heat, add all the ingredients for the teriyaki sauce. Whisk together until the sauce begins to thicken. When thick, set aside.

Place the chicken quarters or sliced tofu onto a large roasting tray with the coconut oil and season to taste. Toss the chicken or tofu, making sure it is evenly coated in the oil. Drizzle a small amount of teriyaki sauce over the chicken or tofu, saving at least half for later. Pop the chicken or tofu into the oven and bake for 12–15 minutes. Remove from the oven, add the remaining teriyaki sauce to the chicken or tofu and toss through.

Place the broccoli, carrots, edamame and pineapple on the roasting tray around the cooked chicken or tofu. Season with black pepper and drizzle with the sesame oil. Pop into the oven for 20 minutes until the chicken or tofu is cooked through. When ready, remove the chicken and cut into strips. Build your bowl with your rice, chicken or tofu, and vegetables. Top with the spring onions and sesame seeds.

FOOD TIP

It's important to be mindful of the food waste we generate in the kitchen. For example, I feel it is unnecessary to peel my carrots, creating waste with the skins, as there is a lot of nutritional value that comes from the peel and the layers just beneath it. Alternatively, start a compost heap and add your peels to that.

FUNGI RISOTTO

PEARL BARLEY MUSHROOM RISOTTO (VEGETARIAN)

SERVES 4

This is a gamechanger in the world of risotto. Risotto is known as a challenging dish as it can often become stodgy or overcooked. The pearl barley is much more forgiving, but don't be fooled. Even though it's much easier to cook than classic risotto, it makes just as much of an impact.

½ CUP PORCINI MUSHROOMS

1 CUP BOILING WATER

6 CUPS VEGETABLE STOCK

COCONUT OIL

1 BROWN ONION, FINELY CHOPPED

2 CLOVES GARLIC, MINCED

2 TABLESPOONS FINELY CHOPPED FRESH
    ROSEMARY LEAVES

1½ CUPS PEARL BARLEY

200 GRAMS EXOTIC MUSHROOMS, SLICED

BLACK PEPPER

½ CUP COCONUT CREAM

¾ CUP FINELY GRATED PARMESAN CHEESE

Soak the porcini mushrooms in the boiling water. Set aside for 15 minutes.

Add the vegetable stock to a medium-sized saucepan over low heat and bring to a slight simmer.

In a separate large saucepan over medium heat, add 1 tablespoon coconut oil. Add the onion and sauté until softened. Add the garlic and fry for another minute.

Remove the porcini mushrooms from their liquid, adding the liquid to the stock pot. Roughly chop the porcinis and add them to the onion and garlic. Add the rosemary and fry for another minute. Then add the pearl barley and fry until the grain becomes slightly toasted.

Add the stock to the barley, one ladleful at a time, stirring often. Once the barley absorbs the liquid, add another ladleful. Continue this process over medium heat.

Meanwhile, in a separate frying pan over high heat, add 1 teaspoon coconut oil. Once the oil is hot, add half the exotic mushrooms. Once the mushrooms are hot and begin to fry, add the remaining mushrooms. Fry the mushrooms for about 10 minutes until golden brown. Add some freshly cracked black pepper. Once the mushrooms are ready, set aside.

Keep adding the stock to the barley. Once it is ready, after 35–40 minutes, add the coconut cream and ½ cup of the Parmesan and fold through. Pop the lid on and let it simmer for 5 minutes. Once ready, add the mushrooms and fold through. Season to taste and top with the remaining Parmesan and enjoy this warm, hearty bowl.

HEALTH FACT

Aside from being a good source of many vitamins and minerals, pearl barley also helps lower cholesterol due to the soluble fibre, beta-glucan.

HOT AND SPICY PORK

PULLED PORK BOWL

SERVES 4

Pulled pork is often associated with rich and sugar-laden barbecue sauces that are unhealthy and a fast track to heartburn. This recipe illustrates that there is always a healthier alternative that can be served with fresh ingredients.

400 GRAMS PORK BELLY

2 TEASPOONS SMOKED PAPRIKA

2 TEASPOONS COCONUT SUGAR

2 TEASPOONS SALT

5 BAY LEAVES

2 CLOVES GARLIC

1 CUP UNCOOKED QUINOA

1 HANDFUL FRESH KALE, STALKS REMOVED
    AND LEAVES TORN

½ CUP SLICED RED CABBAGE

1 AVOCADO, SLICED

1 SMALL CUCUMBER, SLICED

1 HANDFUL FRESH CORIANDER LEAVES,
    CHOPPED

2 JALAPEÑOS, SLICED

SRIRACHA SAUCE

Preheat the oven to 180 °C.

Place the pork in a frying pan, skin-side down. Turn the heat up to medium and cook for 10 minutes. Once the fat has rendered and the skin is crispy brown, turn and cook the other side for another 2 minutes. Once browned, remove from the heat.

In a small bowl, mix together the paprika, coconut sugar and salt and rub all over the pork.

Place a wire rack inside a roasting pan. Fill with 3 cm water. Add the bay leaves and garlic to the water. Place the meat on the rack, cover the pan with foil and pop into the oven for 4 hours. Halfway through, check on the meat. If the water runs too low, top it up.

Meanwhile, cook the quinoa as per packet instructions or refer to page 10.

Once the meat is ready, remove from the roasting pan. Shred the pork using two forks.

To assemble, place the quinoa in a bowl and add the pork. Decorate the bowl using the kale, cabbage, avocado and cucumber. Top with the coriander, jalapeños and sriracha to taste.

HEALTH TIP

Adding chilli to a meal can fire up a sluggish
digestive system and help fight off infections.

HEARTY
HOME BOWLS

Hearty Home Bowls translate into the ultimate comfort food, which is always an easy choice for me. I love selecting a warm and grounded meal to make for a dinner party or even a simple night in. Many of these hearty bowls are wonderful to share with friends or family so feel free to double up on the recipes or pair them with a fresh bowl. They are robust and will leave you feeling full and warm.

Some of these bowls are one-pot wonders, such as the Butternut Curry (see page 92) and the Humble Stew (see page 105), which is ideal as it means I can spend more time enjoying the meal and less time washing dishes. Others are more labour intensive, such as the Lentil Masala (see page 99).

Regardless of prep time, all of them will leave you feeling satisfied and hopefully as nurtured as I do after eating them.

CASABLANCA BOWL

SPICED BAKED CAULIFLOWER (VEGAN)

SERVES 2

The cauliflower is the hero of this dish, even though its preparation is simply having been rubbed with some spices and cooked whole. For many vegetables, if you cook them whole they retain their flavour, providing a more intense taste to your dish.

COCONUT OIL

1 HEAD CAULIFLOWER

1 LARGE ONION, CHOPPED

1 CLOVE GARLIC, MINCED

4 TOMATOES, CHOPPED

1½ CUPS BROWN LENTILS

4 CUPS VEGETABLE STOCK

SALT AND PEPPER

5 MEDJOOL DATES, PITTED AND CHOPPED

40 GRAMS RAW ALMONDS, CHOPPED

1 LARGE HANDFUL FRESH CORIANDER,
    ROUGHLY CHOPPED

SPICE RUB

1 TEASPOON GROUND CUMIN

1 TEASPOON GROUND GINGER

¾ TEASPOON BLACK PEPPER

1 TEASPOON TURMERIC

½ TEASPOON GROUND CORIANDER

½ TEASPOON GROUND CINNAMON

½ TEASPOON CAYENNE PEPPER

1 TEASPOON SALT

Preheat the oven to 180 °C.

In a bowl, combine the spices for the rub and mix together. Make a paste with 2 tablespoons coconut oil and 1 tablespoon of the spice mix, and brush it evenly over the whole cauliflower. Place on a baking tray in the oven and roast for 40 minutes.

Add the onion and 1 tablespoon coconut oil to a medium-sized saucepan over medium heat and cook until translucent. Add the garlic and stir. Mix in 1 tablespoon of the spice mix and let the flavours draw into the onion. Add the tomatoes and stir well for 5 minutes. Add the lentils and stir for another 5 minutes.

Now add the vegetable stock and bring to a simmer. Cover the saucepan and cook for 40 minutes, checking up on it every 10 minutes or so to ensure it's not drying out. If the water level gets low, top up with some boiling water. After 40 minutes the lentils should be soft. Season to taste. Switch the oven off and leave the cauliflower inside until you're ready to serve. You can serve it whole or chop it up. Serve the lentils in a bowl with the cauliflower and top with the dates, almonds and coriander. And feast!

HEALTH TIP

Spices have many medicinal properties and I encourage you to read up about them. Turmeric, for example, has very high anti-inflammatory properties. It will bring light into your life and you can add it to almost everything. This comforting bowl heats you from the inside out. I consider it soul food, so you can enjoy it wholeheartedly. Happy belly. Happy heart.

BUTTERNUT CURRY

BUTTERNUT, CHICKPEA AND LENTIL CURRY (VEGAN)

SERVES 6

I love a one-pot-wonder meal and this butternut curry is a prime example of that. Not only does it deliver on flavour, but it will also leave you with fewer dishes. Unless, of course, you have all of your friends over to share in the magic of dishwashing.

COCONUT OIL

1 BROWN ONION, CHOPPED

2 CLOVES GARLIC, MINCED

1 TABLESPOON GROUND GINGER

1 TABLESPOON GROUND CUMIN

1 TABLESPOON TURMERIC

1½ TEASPOONS CAYENNE PEPPER

2 LARGE LEEKS, SLICED

600 GRAMS BUTTERNUT, PEELED AND
    CUBED

500 GRAMS LENTILS

250 GRAMS COOKED CHICKPEAS

800 MILLILITRES COCONUT MILK

800 GRAMS PLUM TOMATOES, DICED

1 CUP VEGETABLE STOCK

SALT AND PEPPER

1½ CUPS UNCOOKED WILD BROWN RICE

2 HANDFULS FRESH CORIANDER, CHOPPED

In a large saucepan (preferably cast-iron) over medium heat, add 1 tablespoon coconut oil and the onion and fry until translucent. Add the garlic, ginger, cumin, turmeric and cayenne pepper. Fry for a minute or two to release the flavours. If it becomes dry, add a splash of water to help it along into a paste.

Add the leeks, butternut, lentils, chickpeas, coconut milk, tomatoes and vegetable stock. Simmer for 1¼ hours. Keep your eye on it and give it a stir every 10–15 minutes. If it looks like it's drying out, top up with hot water. Season to taste.

While the curry is cooking, cook the rice as per packet instructions or refer to page 10.

Once the rice and curry are ready, serve with freshly chopped coriander.

HEALTH FACT

Did you know that turmeric is a powerful anti-inflammatory and helps the body heal and repair damage? It is also rich in betacarotene and magnesium. Turmeric essential oils can be used for muscle pain, inflammation, as an antifungal and as an antiseptic ointment.

THE SPANIARD

SEAFOOD PAELLA

SERVES 6–8

The first time I tried paella, I was lucky enough to be sitting by the ocean in Barcelona, Spain. It is a moment I will never forget and I hope that the first taste of my paella leaves you with wanderlust to take that flight.

---

250 GRAMS DEBONED CHICKEN THIGHS

⅓ CUP SPELT FLOUR

COCONUT OIL

150 GRAMS CHORIZO SAUSAGE, SLICED (OPTIONAL)

1 TABLESPOON TOMATO PASTE

1 LARGE BROWN ONION, CHOPPED

2 CLOVES GARLIC, MINCED

1 RED CHILLI (OPTIONAL)

2 TEASPOONS SMOKED PAPRIKA

2 PLUM TOMATOES, CHOPPED

2 STALKS CELERY, FINELY CHOPPED

2 HANDFULS FRESH FLAT-LEAF PARSLEY LEAVES, FINELY CHOPPED

8 CUPS CHICKEN STOCK

2 PINCHES SAFFRON THREADS

500 GRAMS UNCOOKED PAELLA RICE (OR RISOTTO)

300 GRAMS SEAFOOD MIX

100 GRAMS DESHELLED AND DEVEINED PRAWNS

1 CUP FRESH OR FROZEN PEAS

SALT AND PEPPER

2 LEMONS, CUT INTO WEDGES

HEALTH FACT

Celery is a low-GI food and very high in vitamin K. It is also an antioxidant with sources such as vitamin C, betacarotene and manganese. Celery can lower cholesterol, inflammation and blood pressure, and can help with bloating and prevent ulcers. Not to mention it adds a great bit of crunch to a bowl.

Preheat the oven to 180 °C.

Dust the chicken thighs with the spelt flour. In a large frying pan over medium heat, add 1 tablespoon coconut oil. Add the chicken thighs and fry until they are golden brown, then pop them into the oven and roast them for 15 minutes or until cooked through. Set aside.

In the same frying pan over medium heat, add the chorizo and fry for 5–10 minutes to release the flavour. When it is golden brown, it is ready. Add the tomato paste to the chorizo. Add the onion, garlic, chilli, paprika, tomatoes, celery, parsley and 2 teaspoons coconut oil. Fry until the onion and celery are soft, stirring often.

Meanwhile, heat the chicken stock in a medium-sized saucepan over medium heat. Add the saffron to the stock.

Add the rice to the frying pan with the chorizo and spices and fry for 5 minutes, stirring continuously. Add a quarter of the saffron-infused stock to the pan and stir. Once the rice begins to absorb the liquid, add another quarter of the stock and keep stirring.

This dish needs a little bit of nurturing – remember that the energy you put into your food is the energy that you will ultimately be putting into your body. Take time to be patient with your food and be mindful in creating it.

Once the paella has absorbed the liquid, add the remaining stock and cover with the lid. Simmer for 20 minutes, stirring occasionally. If the paella dries out, keep feeding it with stock or add a bit of water.

With 10 minutes left, add the seafood mix and combine.

With 5 minutes left, add the chicken thighs, prawns and peas. Stir well and season to taste.

Serve with fresh lemon and treat yourself with a glass of chilled white wine to accompany your paella.

THE MED

MEDITERRANEAN FRIED FALAFEL BOWL (VEGAN)

SERVES 8

What I love about this meal is that you and your friends can get very involved in the eating experience and eat with your hands. You can easily turn this into a mezze feast by adding other elements such as dolmades and roasted red peppers.

2 CUPS FRESH PARSLEY LEAVES, FINELY
   CHOPPED
150 GRAMS ROSA TOMATOES, HALVED
½ RED ONION, DICED
JUICE OF ½ LEMON
1 TABLESPOON TAHINI
1 HANDFUL BABY SPINACH
1 TABLESPOON OLIVE OIL
SALT AND PEPPER
200 GRAMS KALAMATA OR GREEN OLIVES,
   DRAINED
260 GRAMS HUMMUS

FALAFEL

250 GRAMS COOKED CHICKPEAS
½ CUP FRESH PARSLEY LEAVES, CHOPPED
½ CUP CHOPPED BROWN ONION
4 CLOVES GARLIC, SKINS REMOVED
2 TABLESPOONS ROLLED OATS
SALT AND PEPPER
1 TABLESPOON GROUND CUMIN
½ TEASPOON CAYENNE PEPPER
PINCH OF GROUND CARDAMOM
1 TEASPOON GROUND CORIANDER
5 TEASPOONS COCONUT OIL

Add all the falafel ingredients, except the coconut oil, to a food processor and blend until chunky. You still want little pieces of chickpea and parsley showing. If it gets stuck, add a dash of olive oil to help it along. Once ready, place in a bowl in the fridge for 30 minutes.

Meanwhile, in a separate bowl, mix together the parsley, tomatoes, onion, lemon, tahini and baby spinach. Drizzle the olive oil over and season to taste.

Once the falafel mix has set, use a tablespoon to measure out and shape into balls. Spoon them into a hot pan with the coconut oil and fry each one for 2 minutes on each side or until golden brown.

Now for the fun part, it's time to make your meal beautiful. Taking a moment to celebrate the nourishing meal that you have made, assemble your bowl starting with the parsley salad, then the falafels and all the added extras that will make your meal shine. Add the olives and then the hummus. You can use store-bought hummus or go to page 140 for the best hummus ever!

HEALTH FACT

Oats are beneficial for stress and excellent for treating symptoms of fatigue, and auto-immune diseases.

LENTIL MASALA

LENTIL 'MEATBALLS' WITH GARAM MASALA (VEGETARIAN OR VEGAN)

SERVES 4

Learning how to make these meatballs will come in handy because they're also great as an afternoon snack if you keep them in the fridge. They're like little balls of protein so will give you energy at any time of the day.

LENTIL MEATBALLS

1 CUP UNCOOKED BROWN LENTILS

4 CUPS VEGETABLE STOCK

2 TABLESPOONS COCONUT OIL

1 BROWN ONION, CHOPPED

1 CUP GRATED CARROTS

2 CLOVES GARLIC, MINCED

½ CUP ROLLED OATS

1 HANDFUL FRESH FLAT-LEAF PARSLEY

6 FRESH BASIL LEAVES

1½ TABLESPOONS TOMATO PASTE

6 TABLESPOONS FINELY GRATED
   PARMESAN CHEESE (OPTIONAL)

2 TEASPOONS DRIED OREGANO

1 LARGE EGG

MASALA PASTE

1 BROWN ONION

3 CLOVES GARLIC, PEELED

3 CM PIECE FRESH GINGER

1½ TABLESPOONS GARAM MASALA

1 RED OR GREEN CHILLI

½ TABLESPOON TURMERIC

½ TABLESPOON GROUND CUMIN

½ TABLESPOON GROUND CLOVES

1 TEASPOON SALT

2 TEASPOONS CAYENNE PEPPER

1 HANDFUL FRESH CORIANDER, CHOPPED

40 GRAMS RAW ALMONDS

JUICE OF ½ LEMON

SAUCE

1½ CUPS TOMATO PASSATA

1 CUP VEGETABLE STOCK

400 MILLILITRES COCONUT MILK

1 CUP UNCOOKED WILD RICE

In a medium-sized saucepan over medium heat, add the lentils and stock. Bring to a simmer, cover and cook for about 30 minutes until softened. If the liquid runs low, top it up with hot water. If there's any excess liquid once the lentils are cooked, drain and set the lentils aside.

Meanwhile, in a large frying pan over medium heat, add 1 tablespoon of the coconut oil. Add the onion and fry until translucent. Add the carrots and garlic and fry for another 2 minutes, then set aside.

Place the oats, parsley and basil in a food processor and pulse a few times until the oats have broken up. Add the lentils, onion mixture, tomato paste, Parmesan and oregano to the processor and season to taste. Pulse a few times until the mixture has just combined. Add the egg to the mixture or you can use a flaxseed egg (1 tablespoon flaxseed meal and 2½ tablespoons water). Pulse further until the mixture has just combined. You do not want to pulse until smooth, keep it a bit chunky. Set aside in the fridge for 30 minutes or overnight until the mixture has set.

Preheat the oven to 180 °C.

Line a large roasting tray with baking paper. Using a tablespoon, portion out the lentil mix and roll into balls in the palm of your hand. Arrange them into rows and pop them into the oven. Bake for 20 minutes, turning them at the halfway point.

Meanwhile, place all the ingredients for the masala paste into a food processor and blend until smooth. In a deep frying pan over medium heat, add the masala paste and the remaining 1 tablespoon coconut oil. Fry for 2 minutes to release the flavours.

Add the tomato passata and stock to the masala paste and simmer for about 10 minutes until the colour starts to deepen. Add the coconut milk and simmer for another 15 minutes. Remember the longer you simmer for, the better the flavour. Season to taste.

Cook the rice as per packet instructions or refer to page 10.

This is a dish that has taken time. It is a dish that you have put a lot of love and care into. Acknowledge yourself for that and thank yourself for creating this nourishing meal. Build your bowl with your rice and meatballs and top with your delicious garam masala sauce.

POT PIE PARTY

CHICKEN POT PIE

I love this recipe because there is something special about receiving your own individual pot pie. The best part about it is you get your own fair share of pie crust. You can make any filling, such as a vegetable alternative, and use this same crust technique at your next lunch.

4 CHICKEN BREAST FILLETS

COCONUT OIL

1 CUP APPLE CIDER VINEGAR

1 BROWN ONION, CHOPPED

2 CLOVES GARLIC, MINCED

SALT AND PEPPER

2 CUPS BUTTON MUSHROOMS, CHOPPED

1 CUP PEELED AND CHOPPED BUTTERNUT

2 LEEKS, CHOPPED

8 FRESH SAGE LEAVES

2–3 TEASPOONS FRESH THYME LEAVES

2 TABLESPOONS FLOUR

1½ CUPS CHICKEN STOCK

2 CUPS ALMOND MILK

2 TEASPOONS CAYENNE PEPPER

1 CUP FROZEN PEAS

4 TABLESPOONS SALTED BUTTER

1 ROLL PHYLLO PASTRY

Put a medium-sized saucepan over high heat and add the chicken, 4 tablespoons coconut oil and the apple cider vinegar. Simmer for 12 minutes or until the chicken is cooked through. When it's ready, remove it all from the saucepan and set aside to cool. Once cooled, shred the chicken using two forks.

Add 1 teaspoon coconut oil and the onion to a large frying pan over medium heat. Fry for 5 minutes, then add the garlic. Season to taste. Add the mushrooms and fry for 5 minutes. Add the butternut and leeks and fry for 10 minutes or until the butternut is soft when pierced with a fork. Add the sage and thyme to the pan and stir. Add the flour to the pan and stir well, breaking up any lumps. Cook for another minute.

Add the chicken stock and almond milk along with the cayenne pepper. Simmer for 5 minutes, allowing the sauce to reduce and thicken. Remove from the heat and add the peas and shredded chicken. Mix well and season to taste. Divide the mixture between the ramekins.

Preheat the oven to 180 °C. Grease 6 medium ramekins with butter.

Melt the butter in a small saucepan. Lay out the phyllo pastry, one sheet at a time, and brush it with a generous amount of melted butter. The more you use the more golden and crunchy the pastry will become. When the pastry has been brushed, scrunch up the pastry to fit into the top of the ramekins. Repeat this layering process with the remaining pastry.

Pop the pies into the oven and bake for about 30 minutes or until the phyllo is deliciously golden brown.

FOOD TIP

Mindful eating is about connecting your mind and body. There's no point in feeling guilty about the food you're eating, you won't enjoy it and you'll only receive negativity in mind and body. Rather pay attention to how you feel after eating certain foods, release the negative emotions and be present. If you feel sluggish, have brain fog or feel your body crashing, then avoid foods that make you feel that way. No food is worth feeling unwell.

GREEN CURRY

THAI GREEN CURRY WITH QUINOA (MEAT OR VEGAN)

SERVES 4

This is another classic favourite and crowd pleaser. I have coupled it with quinoa rather than rice to give it a protein kick. As delicious as coconut milk is, it can sometimes mute other flavours, so make sure you taste test as you cook and don't be afraid to season it. And, of course, don't forget the squeeze of lime before serving.

GREEN CURRY PASTE

- 4 CLOVES GARLIC, SKINS REMOVED
- 3 STALKS FRESH LEMONGRASS, OUTER LEAVES REMOVED
- 6 CM PIECE FRESH GINGER
- 2 SHALLOTS
- 4 GREEN CHILLIES (OR MORE IF YOU LIKE HEAT)
- 2 HEAPED TEASPOONS GROUND CUMIN
- 1 HANDFUL FRESH CORIANDER LEAVES
- 2 TABLESPOONS FISH SAUCE (VEGAN ALTERNATIVE: SOY SAUCE)

CURRY

- 1 CUP UNCOOKED QUINOA
- 3 CHICKEN BREAST FILLETS (OPTIONAL)
- 100 GRAMS SHIMEJI MUSHROOMS
- 1.2 LITRES COCONUT MILK
- 100 GRAMS SUGAR SNAP PEAS
- 250 GRAMS TENDER-STEM BROCCOLI
- 250 GRAMS PAK CHOI
- 100 GRAMS BABY CORN
- 100 GRAMS BEAN SPROUTS
- SALT AND PEPPER
- 1 HANDFUL FRESH CORIANDER LEAVES
- 2 LIMES, QUARTERED
- TAMARI

In a food processor, add all the ingredients for the paste and blend until almost smooth.

Cook the quinoa as per packet instructions or refer to page 10.

In a small saucepan over high heat, add 1 cup water and the chicken breasts. Bring to the boil, then simmer for 10 minutes or until cooked through. Remove from the heat, let cool and shred with two forks.

In a large saucepan, add the curry paste and fry over medium heat for 5 minutes to release all the flavours. Add the mushrooms and fry for another 5 minutes.

Add the coconut milk and 1 cup water and simmer for 10 minutes, allowing the flavour to develop.

Add the shredded chicken and the sugar snap peas, broccoli, pak choi, baby corn and bean sprouts. Cover the saucepan with a lid and cook for 5 minutes. Season to taste.

Build your bowl with quinoa and the curry and top with freshly chopped coriander, a squeeze of lime and a drizzle of tamari.

HEALTH TIP

Quinoa is one of the great vegetarian complete proteins. It is a wonderful building block for the body, as well as a high-sustenance grain. And it has the extra bonus of being gluten free.

HUMBLE STEW

HEARTY BEEF STEW BOWL

SERVES 4

A classic stew is a good recipe to have in your repertoire. The longer you cook it the better and more tender it becomes. It is wonderful for meal prep as you can pre-portion it and freeze it for meals on the run. Don't limit yourself because you can pack this with almost any vegetable you like.

500 GRAMS BEEF SHIN
1 TABLESPOON SPELT FLOUR
COCONUT OIL
1 BROWN ONION, CHOPPED
2 CLOVES GARLIC, MINCED
5 BAY LEAVES
2–3 TEASPOONS FRESH THYME LEAVES
1 TEASPOON SMOKED PAPRIKA
1 TEASPOON GROUND CINNAMON
2 TEASPOONS CAYENNE PEPPER
2 TABLESPOONS TOMATO PASTE
3 LARGE CARROTS, CHOPPED
1 CUP CHOPPED CELERY
400 GRAMS TOMATOES, DICED
3 CUPS BEEF STOCK
4 LARGE POTATOES, CUBED
1 CUP UNCOOKED BROWN RICE
120 GRAMS TENDER-STEM BROCCOLI
1 HANDFUL SWISS CHARD, STEMS
    REMOVED AND LEAVES TORN

Preheat the oven to 160 °C.

Place the beef shin on a board and sprinkle both sides with the spelt flour. Place the beef shin in a large stovetop-to-oven casserole over medium heat and cook until browned on both sides. Remove from the dish and set aside.

In the same casserole, add 1 tablespoon coconut oil. Add the onion and fry for 5 minutes, stirring often. Add the garlic and fry for another minute. Add the bay leaves and thyme along with the paprika, cinnamon, cayenne pepper and tomato paste and fry for another 2 minutes to release the flavours. Add a dash of water if it looks dry. Using a wooden spoon, add a dash of water to deglaze the bottom of the casserole to mix in all the goodness. Add the carrots and celery and fry for 1 minute. Add the tomatoes, beef stock and browned shin and mix through. Cover with the lid and pop into the oven for 3 hours.

Meanwhile, cook the rice as per packet instructions or refer to page 10.

Once the meat is tender and ready, add the potatoes to the casserole and cook for another 20 minutes. When they are soft, add the broccoli and Swiss chard and fold through.

Adding fresh greens to a hot dish can add a great crunch and is a wonderful way to get in some extra greens.

Remove from the heat and serve the rice and the beef stew together.

FOOD TIP

You can never overcook a stew so long as you keep it hydrated. The longer it cooks, the better it gets. Sometimes it is better the next day so don't forget to keep leftovers for freezing so you can grab it for work to save time and money or use it for dinners throughout the week as food prep. This is a nice way to enjoy slow cooking on the run.

THE NOMAD

WINTER BAKED FALAFEL VEGETABLE BOWL (VEGAN)

SERVES 4

You can't go wrong with roasted vegetables, falafel and hummus. It's one of my favourite dishes and many of my friends agree. I hope you do too!

---

6 MEDIUM-SIZED CARROTS, SLICED

1 HEAD CAULIFLOWER, BROKEN INTO FLORETS

2 TABLESPOONS COCONUT OIL

2 TEASPOONS MUSTARD SEEDS

4 TEASPOONS GROUND CUMIN

SALT AND PEPPER

1 TEASPOON COCONUT OIL

2 CUPS SLICED RED CABBAGE

2 HANDFULS BABY SPINACH

¼ CUP PISTACHIOS, SHELLED

1 JALAPEÑO, SLICED

FALAFEL

2 CUPS UNCOOKED BROWN LENTILS

1 GENEROUS HANDFUL FRESH CORIANDER

1 GENEROUS HANDFUL FRESH PARSLEY

½ JALAPEÑO

2 TABLESPOONS COCONUT OIL

2 CLOVES GARLIC

JUICE OF ½ LEMON

1 TEASPOON GROUND CUMIN

2 TABLESPOONS ROLLED OATS

SALT AND PEPPER

DRESSING

1 TEASPOON HONEY

¼ CUP OLIVE OIL

1 TABLESPOON TAHINI

JUICE OF ½ LEMON

SALT AND PEPPER

Preheat the oven to 180 °C.

Keep the oven on for the duration of this recipe as you are going to use it later for the falafels.

Place the carrots, cauliflower, coconut oil, mustard seeds and cumin on a large roasting tray. Toss the vegetables until they are covered with the spices and oil. Season to taste and pop them into the oven for 30 minutes or until the edges become crispy. Don't forget to toss them at the halfway mark. Once ready, remove from the oven and set aside.

For the falafel, cook the lentils as per packet instructions or refer to page 10. Once ready, drain and set aside to cool.

In a food processor, pulse together all the falafel ingredients. Do not pulse until smooth, as you want the falafels to have texture. You want to create the texture of a crumble. Set aside in the fridge for 10 minutes to set.

Meanwhile, line a large roasting tray with baking paper. Once the falafel mixture has set, remove from the fridge and form golf-ball-sized patties. Place the patties in rows on a roasting tray and pop them into the oven for 18 minutes, turning them at the halfway mark.

In a bowl, combine all the ingredients for the dressing and set aside.

In a medium-sized frying pan over high heat, add 1 teaspoon coconut oil. Add the cabbage and sauté for 4 minutes.

Build the bowl by layering the spinach, cabbage, roasted vegetables and falafels. Top with the pistachios, jalapeño and dressing. If you would like an extra touch, serve with hummus (see page 140).

HEALTH TIP

Jalapeños can relieve nasal congestion and headaches, and aid weight loss.

LABOUR OF LOVE

CHEESY AUBERGINE PARMIGIANO (VEGETARIAN)

SERVES 6–8

This is along the lines of a traditional parmigiano, but if you wish to layer different vegetables such as courgettes, spinach or mushrooms, you can create a delicious vegetable bake. It'll only get better because of all the nutrients you've packed in.

1 LARGE BROWN ONION, CHOPPED

1 CLOVE GARLIC, MINCED

2–3 TEASPOONS FRESH ROSEMARY LEAVES

COCONUT OIL

8 PLUM TOMATOES, CHOPPED

400 GRAMS CHERRY TOMATOES, DICED

1 HANDFUL FRESH BASIL, CHOPPED

350 GRAMS TOMATO PASSATA

SALT AND PEPPER

1 RED CHILLI OR CAYENNE PEPPER
    (OPTIONAL)

2 LARGE AUBERGINES, SLICED
    LENGTHWAYS

100 GRAMS PARMESAN CHEESE, FINELY
    GRATED

300 GRAMS MOZZARELLA CHEESE, SLICED

In a medium-sized saucepan over medium heat, add the onion, garlic, rosemary and 1 teaspoon coconut oil and fry until translucent. Add the plum and cherry tomatoes, basil and passata and mix well. Cover with a lid and simmer for 1–1¼ hours. Season to taste.

Keep an eye on it. If it dries out, add a little water. The longer you cook any tomato-based dish, the sweeter and less acidic it becomes. This helps you skip the trick of adding sugar to the tomato sauce. If you want to add a little heat, feel free to add a red chilli or a sprinkle of cayenne pepper.

In a frying pan over medium to high heat, add 1 tablespoon coconut oil. Once the oil has heated, add the aubergine slices and fry for 3 minutes per side. Aubergine absorbs oil, so don't add more if the slices seem dry because if there is too much oil once it's cooked it will become soggy. Once the aubergines are ready, set aside.

Preheat the oven to 180 °C.

To assemble the parmigiano, layer the ingredients in an ovenproof lasagne dish. Start with the tomato sauce, then the aubergine slices, then the Parmesan and repeat, ending off with the tomato sauce. Top the dish evenly with the mozzarella slices and a handful of Parmesan. Pop it in the oven for 20 minutes or until the cheese is melted and beautiful. Once it's ready, allow to cool for 10 minutes before serving. You can put some square pegs in round holes here by cutting it into rectangles and putting it in bowls.

FOOD TIP

The tomato sauce from this dish is a great base and is good to have in your repertoire. It can be used as the base for a pasta or lasagne, on top of scrambled eggs for breakfast, or to add a bit of heat to a Mexican dish. You can add a bit of sweetness to balance the acidity or balance it naturally by grating in some carrots. Also remember that the longer a tomato sauce cooks, the sweeter it gets.

OODLES OF NOODLES

Pasta is often demonised and avoided because of the 'carbs are bad' label. I know I have dealt with feelings of guilt after eating a pasta dish, which has been counter-productive to my health goals.

Thankfully, I have managed to shift my mindset and believe that pasta is most certainly acceptable in moderation, and this has in turn allowed me to test out healthier options and recipes which include pasta variations.

Releasing negative thoughts is definitely the way to a healthier lifestyle.

I have really enjoyed seeing how many healthy and delicious alternatives there are to the common wheat pasta. Only one recipe in this chapter has a wheat pasta as the base, the rest are all made from different flours and grains.

I encourage you to try and make your own pasta if you have the time and the tools. Discover and play around with different ingredients and alternatives; when you are in the store and about to buy the classic spaghetti, pause, have a look around, and see if you can find a chickpea, spelt or wholewheat alternative. I also absolutely love rice noodles – they are great in soups and broths or with a simple stir-fry.

If you find that gluten-rich foods don't make you feel like you're at your optimal strength and clarity, then see if gluten-free options work better for you. Just don't be scared of making and eating a pasta dish, because not all pastas are created equal, and these oodles of noodles are both delicious and packed with nutrition!

MAMMA MIA

MEATBALL AND CHICKPEA PASTA

SERVES 6

I love making meatballs with a tomato sauce. You can serve them as a tapas on a Spanish-themed evening or with a pasta as done in this recipe.

SAUCE

- 1 TABLESPOON COCONUT OIL
- 1 RED ONION, FINELY CHOPPED
- 1 CLOVE GARLIC, MINCED
- 1 TEASPOON DRIED OREGANO
- 1 TEASPOON CAYENNE PEPPER
- 500 GRAMS ROSA TOMATOES, HALVED
- 6 PLUM TOMATOES, DICED
- 2 TABLESPOONS BALSAMIC VINEGAR

MEATBALLS

- 1 TABLESPOON COCONUT OIL
- ½ BROWN ONION, CHOPPED
- 1 CLOVE GARLIC, MINCED
- 1 TEASPOON DRIED OREGANO
- ½ GREEN CHILLI
- 1 HANDFUL FRESH PARSLEY LEAVES, ROUGHLY CHOPPED
- ¼ CUP DRIED BREADCRUMBS
- 800 GRAMS BEEF MINCE
- 2 EGGS
- ⅓ CUP FINELY GRATED PARMESAN CHEESE, PLUS EXTRA FOR SERVING
- SALT AND PEPPER

- 250 GRAMS CHICKPEA PASTA (OR A PASTA SUBSTITUTE OF YOUR CHOICE)
- OLIVE OIL FOR DRIZZLING
- FRESH BASIL LEAVES FOR SERVING

HEALTH TIP

Try to be mindful of your decisions when buying food. Think about what you buy or eat. For example, chickpea pasta is a great alternative to wheat pasta and is high in protein. These little actions add up and can result in a healthier, balanced life!

Make the sauce first. In a large frying pan over medium heat, add the coconut oil and onion and fry for about 5 minutes until translucent. Add the garlic, oregano and cayenne pepper and stir. Add all the tomatoes and the balsamic vinegar.

Fry for 10 minutes, stirring often. If it dries out, add a dash of water. Turn down the heat, pop the lid on and let it simmer for 45 minutes. Check up on the sauce every now and again and add a dash of water if needed. You don't want it to lose all of its moisture.

While the sauce is cooking, make the meatballs. In a medium-sized frying pan over medium heat, add the coconut oil and the onion and fry for 5 minutes. Add the garlic, oregano and chilli and fry for another 4 minutes, stirring often. Take off the heat and set aside.

Preheat the oven to 180 °C. Lightly grease a large roasting tray.

In a large bowl, add the parsley, breadcrumbs and the beef. Using a fork, break up the mince. Add the eggs, Parmesan and cooked onion and season to taste. Using your hands, mix all the ingredients together. Don't overwork the meat as the meatballs will become tough. Mix so that the ingredients are just combined.

Using a tablespoon, measure out the mixture into equal-sized balls. Roll them around in your hands and place them on the greased roasting tray. Pop them in the oven and bake for 30 minutes or until they are cooked through.

Ten minutes before the meatballs are ready, cook the pasta as per packet instructions. Don't overcook the pasta as it will cook further when added to the tomato sauce. Once done, drain the pasta and give it a good glug of olive oil so it doesn't stick together.

Once everything is ready, mix the sauce and pasta together and top with the meatballs. Serve with some fresh basil and grated Parmesan!

COCONUT NOODLES

COCONUT BROTH WITH GREEN TEA CHICKEN (MEAT OR VEGAN)

SERVES 4

*This coconut broth is very soothing and the green tea chicken is a fun technique to experiment
with and adds a new element of flavour to the dish.*

1.6 LITRES COCONUT MILK

400 MILLILITRES WATER

4 STALKS FRESH LEMONGRASS

4 TEASPOONS GRATED FRESH GINGER

1 GREEN CHILLI, CHOPPED (OR MORE IF
YOU LIKE LOTS OF HEAT)

2 CLOVES GARLIC, MINCED

1 SHALLOT, DICED

2 HANDFULS FRESH CORIANDER LEAVES

150 GRAMS EXOTIC MUSHROOMS

3 GREEN TEA BAGS

2 CHICKEN BREAST FILLETS (OPTIONAL)

200 GRAMS RICE VERMICELLI (OR EGG
NOODLE OF YOUR CHOICE)

230 GRAMS TENDER-STEM BROCCOLI

60 GRAMS SUGAR SNAP PEAS

60 GRAMS BABY CORN

160 GRAMS PAK CHOI

2 LIMES

In a large saucepan over medium heat, add all the coconut milk and water. Crush the lemongrass to release the flavour and add it to the saucepan. Then add the ginger, chilli, garlic and shallot. Add one handful of the coriander leaves and bring to a simmer for 20 minutes. Don't let the broth boil.

Once ready, strain and discard the solids, saving the coconut milk broth. The broth is now flavoured. Pop it back on the stove over a low heat and add the mushrooms.

Meanwhile, fill a small saucepan with water, place over medium heat and bring to a boil. Turn down the heat to the lowest it can go and add the tea bags. Let steep for 2 minutes. Remove the tea bags and add the chicken. Cover with a lid and poach the chicken for 12 minutes or until cooked through. Once ready, remove the chicken and slice it into bite-sized pieces.

If the noodles need to be soaked in water for 10 minutes, then do so now and then drain.

Add the chicken, broccoli, sugar snap peas, baby corn, pak choi and noodles to the broth. Turn the heat up for 4 minutes. Remove from the heat and serve with the remaining chopped coriander leaves and freshly squeezed lime juice.

HEALTH FACT

Chilli triggers pain signals that are transmitted to the brain. These signals cause the brain to release endorphins, which are natural pain killers that create a feeling of wellbeing.

TWO VEG PASTA

BURNT BUTTER AND SAGE SPELT PASTA WITH BROCCOLI (VEGETARIAN)

SERVES 2

Next time you are making a dish and trying to squeeze in some extra greens, simply grate in a head of raw broccoli.
I do this with my pastas, as is the case here, and occasionally with my grain bowls.

---

400 GRAMS BUTTERNUT, PEELED AND
    CUBED
1 TABLESPOON COCONUT OIL
SALT AND PEPPER
2 CUPS SPELT PENNE (OR PASTA
    SUBSTITUTE OF YOUR CHOICE)
OLIVE OIL
½ HEAD BROCCOLI
80 GRAMS BUTTER
½ RED CHILLI, CHOPPED
¼ CUP FRESH SAGE LEAVES
½ CUP FINELY GRATED PARMESAN CHEESE
¼ CUP PINE NUTS

Preheat the oven to 180 °C.

Place the butternut and coconut oil in a roasting tray. Toss until evenly covered and season with salt and pepper. Roast in the oven for 40 minutes or until soft and golden brown. Set aside.

Bring a medium-sized saucepan of salted water to a boil. Add the penne and cook for 7 minutes, then drain and add a dash of olive oil.

Using a grater, grate the broccoli head and discard the stems.

In a large frying pan, add the butter and chilli. Turn the heat up to medium and wait for the butter to brown. Turn down the heat and add the sage leaves. As they begin to crisp, add the pasta and most of the Parmesan, and fold through. Add the butternut and grated broccoli and toss. Serve topped with pine nuts and the rest of the Parmesan. Season to taste and enjoy.

HEALTH TIP

Pine nuts are a great source of magnesium, low levels of which can cause fatigue. They also contain monounsaturated fats, which are good for heart health.

RA-RA-RAMEN

DUCK RAMEN

SERVES 2

Sometimes the pleasure lies in how you eat, and this ramen dish is a great example of that. Slurping down your noodles can be immensely satisfying and bring a lot of joy and laughter, as well as being delicious!

2 TABLESPOONS WHITE MISO PASTE

2 TABLESPOONS TAMARI

3 WHOLE STAR ANISE

5 CM PIECE FRESH GINGER, THINLY SLICED

2 CLOVES GARLIC, CRUSHED

½ RED CHILLI, FINELY CHOPPED

4 CUPS CHICKEN STOCK

SALT AND PEPPER

200 GRAMS EGG NOODLES

2 DUCK BREAST FILLETS

2 EGGS

1 GENEROUS HANDFUL PAK CHOI

½ CUP SLICED RED CABBAGE

1 HANDFUL FRESH CORIANDER LEAVES, ROUGHLY CHOPPED

SESAME SEEDS

In a medium-sized saucepan over medium heat, add the miso paste and fry for 1 minute. Add the tamari, star anise, ginger, garlic and chilli. Fry for another minute. Add the chicken stock, season and bring to a gentle simmer while you prepare the rest of the ingredients.

Cook the noodles as per packet instructions. Once ready, set aside.

Bring a small saucepan of water to a boil. You will need this for the eggs.

While the water is coming to a boil, add the duck breasts to a medium-sized frying pan over medium heat. You want the duck breasts to get hot with the pan. Let the duck cook for 10 minutes, skin-side down, to crisp the skin and cook out the fat. Once the skin is golden brown, turn the duck and cook for another 3–4 minutes. Once ready, remove from the heat and place on a board. Cover with foil and let it rest for 5 minutes.

While the duck is resting, pop the eggs into the boiling water. Six minutes will give you the perfect gooey egg. Once ready, place the eggs in ice water to stop the cooking process. This also helps ease the peeling process. Peel and slice the eggs.

Place the pak choi, cabbage and noodles in your serving bowls. Strain the broth, keeping the liquid and discarding the solids. Add the liquid to your bowls using a ladle. Slice the duck and add it with the eggs to the bowls.

Top with the coriander and sesame seeds and season to taste.

HEALTH TIP

Red cabbage protects against Alzheimer's and other cognitive disorders. It also promotes good skin health.

ROSEMARY'S BAKE

THE BEST VEGETARIAN LASAGNE (VEGETARIAN)

SERVES 6

This is a very special dish that is near and dear to my heart. It was first made for me by my friend Rose, who has been a big inspiration in my vegetarian cooking. Her original dish was called the Lasagn-Yoh, but after a few changes and flavour additions, this was the result. So it is fitting that it is named after her.

COCONUT OIL

1 RED ONION, CHOPPED

2 CLOVES GARLIC, FINELY CHOPPED

2-3 TEASPOONS FRESH THYME LEAVES

700 GRAMS ROSA TOMATOES, HALVED

700 MILLILITRES TOMATO PASSATA

50 GRAMS FRESH BASIL LEAVES, CHOPPED

SALT AND PEPPER

1 LARGE BUTTERNUT, PEELED AND
    CHOPPED

1 TEASPOON BUTTER

400 GRAMS PORTABELLINI MUSHROOMS,
    SLICED

2-3 TEASPOONS FRESH ROSEMARY LEAVES

1 CUP COCONUT CREAM (OR REGULAR
    CREAM)

1 LARGE AUBERGINE, SLICED INTO DISCS

200 GRAMS SWISS CHARD, ROUGHLY
    CHOPPED

ZEST OF 1 LEMON

300 GRAMS FRESH RICOTTA CHEESE

250 GRAMS EGG LASAGNE SHEETS (OR A
    SUBSTITUTE OF YOUR CHOICE)

450 GRAMS MOZZARELLA CHEESE, SLICED

½ CUP GRATED PARMESAN CHEESE

HEALTH TIP

Swiss chard, like baby spinach, is an alkaline food, which boosts strength. It builds your immune system and helps keep bones healthy. It also helps to regulate blood pressure, so stuff as much in there as you can!

Preheat the oven to 180 °C.

In a large saucepan over medium heat, add 1 tablespoon coconut oil and the onion and garlic and fry until translucent. Add the thyme and tomatoes and fry until soft. Add the tomato passata and basil and simmer. The longer the tomato sauce simmers, the sweeter the sauce becomes. I simmer for almost 2 hours if I can, but 45 minutes should do the trick. Season to taste.

Put the butternut on a roasting tray and lightly coat with ½ tablespoon coconut oil. Sprinkle on salt and roast for 35–40 minutes or until soft. When it is ready, remove from the oven but keep the oven on.

In a small frying pan over medium to high heat, add the butter and mushrooms and fry for about 10 minutes until they are golden brown. Add the rosemary and fry for another minute. Add half the cream to the pan. Let it simmer for 1 minute, then remove from the heat and set aside.

In a large frying pan over high heat, add ½ tablespoon coconut oil. Once hot, add your discs of aubergine. Fry for about 3 minutes on each side until golden brown (add a little more oil if needed) and then set aside.

In a large mixing bowl, add the Swiss chard and lemon zest. Crumble the ricotta into the bowl and toss with the Swiss chard.

Add the butternut to a large lasagne dish and pat down to make a compact flat layer. Top with four ladles of tomato sauce. Add the lasagne sheets by lining them up next to each other to make one even layer. You do not need to soak the lasagne first, it will cook out when you bake the dish.

Add the mushrooms on top of the lasagne layer. Smooth out to all corners of the dish. Add the Swiss chard on top. Pack it down and get as much in as you can. It wilts when you bake it so won't take up nearly as much space.

Now add another layer of lasagne sheets followed by a layer of aubergine discs. Assemble it so that it makes a full layer. Cover with the rest of the tomato sauce and then pour over the rest of the cream. Finally cover with the mozzarella slices. Don't be shy and make sure you don't miss a spot. Sprinkle half the Parmesan over the top.

Bake for 35–40 minutes. Keep an eye on the cheese so it doesn't burn, but let it get a bit crispy. Serve with an extra sprinkling of Parmesan.

DRUNKEN DUCK RAGU

DUCK RAGU WITH GNOCCHI

SERVES 4

This is a labour of love and a slow-cooked creation. Take your time when making the gnocchi, and remember it takes practice.
The nonas in Italy did not become pasta masters overnight.

DUCK RAGU

- 800 GRAMS DUCK PIECES
- 1 BROWN ONION, CHOPPED
- 1 CUP CHOPPED CELERY
- 1 CUP CHOPPED CARROTS
- 3 CLOVES GARLIC, MINCED
- 70 GRAMS PANCETTA, ROUGHLY CHOPPED
- 4 BAY LEAVES
- 1 CUP PINOT NOIR
- 800 GRAMS PLUM TOMATOES, DICED
- 1 CUP CHICKEN STOCK
- 1 TEASPOON CHINESE FIVE SPICE
- 2–3 TEASPOONS FRESH ROSEMARY LEAVES
- ½ CUP GREEN OLIVES, PITTED
- 1 HANDFUL FRESH PARSLEY LEAVES, CHOPPED

GNOCCHI

- ABOUT 8 LARGE POTATOES
- ¼ CUP COARSE SALT
- 4 EGG YOLKS
- ⅔ CUP FINELY GRATED PARMESAN CHEESE
- PINCH SALT AND PEPPER
- 2 TEASPOONS GROUND NUTMEG
- 1 TEASPOON LEMON ZEST
- ¾–1 CUP FLOUR

HEALTH TIP

Rosemary has been known to improve
memory and relieve muscle aches. I use
rosemary very liberally as an aromatic in
many of my dishes so don't be shy to use it.

Preheat the oven to 120 °C.

In a large stovetop-to-oven casserole over medium to high heat, add the duck. You don't need oil as the duck will release fat. Cook until golden brown, stirring often, for about 10 minutes. Remove the duck and set aside. Pour off the fat from the casserole, saving about 1 tablespoon for later.

To the casserole, add the onion, celery, carrots, garlic and pancetta. Cook for about 10 minutes over medium heat, stirring often, until the vegetables begin to soften. Add the bay leaves and pinot noir and deglaze.

Return the duck to the casserole along with the tomatoes and stock. Season with the Chinese five spice and rosemary and top with the olives. Cover and bake in the oven for 4 hours, until the duck is tender. Remove the duck using tongs, then discard all the bones and shred the meat.

Return the liquid in the casserole to the stovetop and simmer for another 20 minutes, skimming any excess fat from the top. Return the shredded meat to the casserole and fold through.

When the ragu has about an hour left in the oven, start preparing the gnocchi. Adjust the oven temperature to 180 °C.

In a large saucepan, add the potatoes and cover with water. Bring to a boil for about 15 minutes. You should be able to pierce them with a fork but they should still be firm. Spread the coarse salt on a large roasting tray. Pop the potatoes on top of the salt and roast for 20 minutes. Cool for 10–15 minutes, then halve them, scoop out the insides, and then pass through a sieve or potato ricer. On a clean surface, form the sieved potato lightly together and make a well in the middle. Add the yolks, most of the Parmesan, salt, pepper, nutmeg and lemon zest. Work together until combined.

Add the flour in stages until you are able to roll the gnocchi into sausages. Cut into bite-sized pieces. Gently use a fork to make indentations on the gnocchi pieces. This will help the sauce stick to it.

Poach the gnocchi in simmering salted water for 1–2 minutes until they float to the surface, then remove them. Do not boil them as they will break apart.

Once the gnocchi is ready, pop it in serving bowls and cover with the ragu. Top with the remaining Parmesan and a sprinkle of parsley and serve.

EASY GREEN

SERVES 2

This is a quick and simple recipe. It highlights how healthy eating doesn't have to be complicated or limited to a salad. Appreciate the individual flavours in this dish. You can find great healthy pastas or pasta alternatives at your local health store, for example, chickpea pasta. Give some of them a try for alternatives to regular wheat pasta.

---

200 GRAMS SPINACH TAGLIATELLE (OR
    EGG TAGLIATELLE)
200 GRAMS HALLOUMI CHEESE
SALT AND PEPPER
2 TABLESPOONS PINE NUTS OR CRUSHED
    CASHEW NUTS

GREMOLATA

JUICE OF 1 LEMON
1 HANDFUL FRESH FLAT-LEAF PARSLEY
    LEAVES
3 CLOVES GARLIC
¼ CUP OLIVE OIL
SALT

Add all the ingredients for the gremolata and salt to taste to a food processor and blend until smooth.

Bring a saucepan of salted water to a boil and cook the pasta as per packet instructions or until al dente.

Slice the halloumi into 5-mm-thick slices and fry over medium to high heat, in a non-stick pan, for roughly 1 minute per side or until golden brown. Set aside.

When the pasta is ready, drain and return to the saucepan. Add the gremolata and mix well. Season to taste with salt and a crack of black pepper. Serve hot and topped with the fried halloumi and the pine or cashew nuts.

HEALTH TIP

Simple food is linked to mindful eating. When a dish has few ingredients it really allows you to appreciate each of the flavours. Build a relationship with each ingredient so that you intuitively choose what you eat based on what you need at the time. Listen to your body. Sometimes less is more.

LEMON BEAN PASTA

ARTICHOKE AND BRIE LINGUINI (VEGETARIAN)

SERVES 5

Life is about balance. Sometimes you go to gym and sometimes you eat this pasta on the couch. It is an indulgent pasta to be saved for special occasions. If you would like to add chicken to this recipe it will pair wonderfully.

COCONUT OIL

3 TABLESPOONS PINE NUTS OR CRUSHED
   CASHEW NUTS

3 CLOVES GARLIC, MINCED

250 GRAMS MARINATED ARTICHOKES

1 RED CHILLI, SLICED (OPTIONAL)

SALT AND PEPPER

450 GRAMS WHOLEGRAIN LINGUINI

2 GENEROUS HANDFULS SWISS CHARD,
   CHOPPED

¼ CUP MASCARPONE

250 GRAMS BRIE CHEESE, CUBED

ZEST AND JUICE OF 1 LEMON

200 GRAMS BUTTER BEANS, COOKED

¼ CUP FRESH BASIL LEAVES

OLIVE OIL

In a large frying pan over low to medium heat, add 1 tablespoon coconut oil and the nuts, garlic, artichokes and chilli. Season to taste and fry until the artichokes start to caramelise. Keep an eye on the nuts as they can burn quickly.

Meanwhile, bring a large saucepan of salted water to a boil. Add the pasta and cook for 8–10 minutes or until al dente. Drain the pasta, saving 1 cup of the water. Return the pasta to the saucepan over medium heat, add the Swiss chard, mascarpone, Brie, lemon zest and juice, butter beans and ¼ cup of the saved water (add more if needed). Add the basil and the artichoke mixture and stir together until well combined. Give it a good glug of olive oil, season to taste and serve hot.

HEALTH FACT

Artichokes can boost the immune system and are great for balancing acidity in the body.

THE ROMAN

ROMANESCO AND BASIL PESTO PASTA (VEGETARIAN)

SERVES 2

This pasta is delicious because Romanesco has a nutty flavour and is crunchier than broccoli and cauliflower when sautéed. The texture contrast of the soft pasta with the crunchy vegetable and nuts makes for a perfect mouthful every time.

---

1 TEASPOON COCONUT OIL

1 HEAD ROMANESCO OR BROCCOLI, BROKEN INTO FLORETS

SALT AND PEPPER

250 GRAMS SPINACH PASTA (OR PASTA SUBSTITUTE OF YOUR CHOICE)

1 GENEROUS HANDFUL BABY SPINACH

¼ CUP BASIL PESTO (SEE PAGE 52)

OLIVE OIL

ZEST AND JUICE OF ½ LEMON

GRATED OR SHAVED PARMESAN CHEESE FOR SERVING

40 GRAMS PINE NUTS, TOASTED

Bring a medium-sized saucepan of salted water to a boil.

In a medium-sized frying pan over high heat, add the coconut oil. Add the Romanesco florets and lightly sauté until golden brown. You still want the crunch so don't overdo it. Season to taste and set aside.

Add the pasta to the boiling water and cook for 8 minutes or until al dente. Once ready, drain and return to the saucepan.

Add the spinach, basil pesto and a good glug of olive oil to the pasta. Cover with the lid for 1 minute, allowing the steam to wilt the spinach. Add the Romanesco along with the lemon zest and juice. Toss together until well combined and season to taste.

Serve topped with Parmesan and the freshly toasted pine nuts.

HEALTH TIP

Romanesco is known as the Roman cauliflower. It is a bright and striking green vegetable with a nutty flavour. If you cannot find Romanesco you can substitute with broccoli, but I encourage you to try and find it because it is both delicious and a unique centrepoint to this dish.

TABLE BOWLS

I'm all about people coming together over food and sharing their discoveries and cooking creations. My healthy food journey began in the kitchen, cooking with my friends. We are constantly inspiring each other with new ingredients and flavour combinations. There's a lot that you can learn from the people you surround yourself with.

I have certainly been influenced by my friends, who all happen to be the strongest and most inspirational women I know.

Table bowl food is about creating an abundance of delicious food to share with the people you love.

These table bowls are for sharing. They comprise side dishes, dips, starters, snacks ... you name it. If it's meant for sharing, you'll find it here.

Some of the sides are great for complementing other dishes. For example, the Aztec Gold corn salsa (see page 139) and Hola Guac guacamole (see page 136) can be added as a complementary dish to Frida's Fiesta (see page 81) in the ancient grains chapter, or anywhere else you feel it would be suitable.

The guacamole, hummus and pesto can be used as dips, added to a variety of meals or kept in the fridge for later when you need a snack.

I have more dinner parties than is probably necessary because I love to make a few dishes and share them, harvest-table style. So try a few of these for your pre-dinner snacks or let them shine as a delicious part of your main meal.

THE HEALTH GRILL

MARINATED GRILLED VEGETABLE SALAD (VEGAN)

SERVES 4

This recipe is versatile because you can substitute and add different vegetables. You can add broccoli, tomatoes or cauliflower. Connect with flavours and cooking techniques and let your intuition guide you towards wholesome creations.

SALAD

6 BABY BEETROOTS

1 LARGE AUBERGINE, HALVED AND SLICED
   LENGTHWAYS

SALT

2 LARGE OR 4 SMALL COURGETTES, SLICED
   LENGTHWAYS

2 LARGE BROWN MUSHROOMS, SLICED

1 RED PEPPER

1 YELLOW PEPPER

150 GRAMS GREEN BEANS, BLANCHED

DRESSING

1 LARGE HANDFUL FRESH BASIL LEAVES

1 LARGE HANDFUL FRESH PARSLEY

1 SMALL HANDFUL FRESH MINT LEAVES

1 CLOVE GARLIC, CRUSHED

1 TABLESPOON WHOLEGRAIN MUSTARD

2 TEASPOONS HONEY

½ CUP OLIVE OIL

¼ CUP RED WINE VINEGAR

1 RED CHILLI, FINELY CHOPPED
   (OPTIONAL)

SALT AND PEPPER

Bring a medium-sized saucepan of water to a boil. Add the beetroots and boil for about 20 minutes until soft when pierced with a fork. Once ready, allow to cool. Peel the beetroots and halve them. Set aside once ready.

Lay the aubergine slices on paper towel, sprinkle with salt and let sit for 10 minutes. This is to remove excess moisture and bitterness from the aubergines.

Heat a griddle pan over medium to high heat. Once hot, get ready to grill your vegetables, starting with the aubergines. Pat them dry and grill on both sides until grill lines appear and the aubergines are cooked. Remove from the heat and set aside to cool.

Next, grill the courgettes on one side for about 2 minutes, then set aside to cool. Grill the mushrooms on both sides until grill marks appear, then set aside.

Finally, grill both the peppers whole in the pan, turning until all sides are nicely charred. When done, place in a bowl and immediately cover with clingfilm. This will steam the skins, making the peppers easier to peel. Once cool, peel and remove the core and seeds, and slice the flesh into juicy lengths. (Tip: try to save the juice from the roasted peppers to add to the dressing.)

For the dressing, finely chop all the herbs and the garlic. In a bowl add the mustard, honey, olive oil, red wine vinegar, chilli, chopped herbs and garlic, and any residual pepper juices. Mix well and season to taste.

Finally, prepare a large salad bowl to assemble. Add all the grilled vegetables, the beetroots and green beans to the bowl and pour over the dressing. Toss together and leave to stand for 15 minutes before serving.

HEALTH TIP

Eating a range of colourful vegetables feeds your body with a multitude of nutrients, as colours in fruits and vegetables usually mean different vitamins and health benefits. Vegetables are high in fibre, which can aid in stabilising blood sugar levels.

THYME FOR CEVICHE

TUNA CEVICHE AND CORN CHIPS

SERVES 2

This recipe is simple, quick and healthy. Focus on buying ethically caught tuna, as certain species of tuna are highly endangered and on the red list. Serve on bruschetta with slices of avo and rocket, or mix through some leaves and turn it into a lovely starter. Or try the corn chips option below.

320 GRAMS TUNA

ZEST OF 1 ORANGE

ZEST AND JUICE OF 1 LEMON

⅓ CUP FINELY CHOPPED RED ONION

¼ CUP CAPERS, RINSED AND FINELY CHOPPED

¼ CUP FINELY CHOPPED GREEN PEPPER

¼ CUP FRESH THYME LEAVES (OR LEMON THYME)

OLIVE OIL

SALT AND PEPPER

CORN CHIPS OR CHOPPED ALMONDS

Prepare the tuna by rinsing under cold water. Dice the tuna into 5 mm cubes and add to a medium-sized bowl. Make sure it's a good cut of fish, with minimal connective tissue so that there is no wastage.

Add the orange zest, lemon zest and juice, red onion, capers, green pepper and thyme leaves. Add a splash of olive oil, just enough to get the aromatics to mix evenly through the tuna.

Season well with salt and pepper and chill in the fridge until ready to serve. The longer it rests the more the flavours will infuse and the better it will taste.

I love to shovel it into my mouth with some corn chips, because I can never get enough of it! As a healthier option, use almonds instead of corn chips for that extra crunch.

HEALTH TIP

Tuna is a high-protein food. Protein feeds every cell in your body and is an important part of a balanced diet. Always be mindful of where you source your fish from and make sure it is not endangered and is sustainably caught. If you don't know where your food comes from, then how do you know if it will benefit your body or do more harm than good?

HOLA GUAC!

GUACAMOLE BOWL (VEGAN)

This recipe can be doubled or even tripled depending on how many people are going to share in the fun. Guacamole is not only awesome for a Mexican-themed night, served chilled, but also makes for a delicious snack to help curb any cravings. Best served with corn chips for dipping. You can also add it to other dishes such as Frida's Fiesta (see page 81) in the Ancient Grains chapter.

---

2 AVOCADOS

JUICE OF 1 LEMON

150 GRAMS ROSA TOMATOES, QUARTERED

50 GRAMS RAW ALMONDS, ROUGHLY
   CHOPPED

1 HANDFUL FRESH CORIANDER LEAVES,
   FINELY CHOPPED

1 SMALL RED ONION, FINELY CHOPPED

3 TABLESPOONS OLIVE OIL

1 TABLESPOON BALSAMIC VINEGAR

1 RED CHILLI, CHOPPED (OPTIONAL)

SALT AND PEPPER

Add the avocado and lemon juice to a large mixing bowl. Using a fork, finely mash the avocado. Add the tomatoes, almonds, coriander, onion, olive oil, balsamic, chilli, and salt and pepper to taste and mix well. And that's it! Easy and delicious.

HEALTH TIP

Avocados are high in monounsaturated fats, which protect against heart disease and give flexibility to joints. They are also good for a variety of skin problems, so look up an avo mask while you're mashing up your avos for the guacamole.

AZTEC GOLD

GRILLED CRUNCHY CORN SALSA (VEGAN)

This is a great accompaniment to spicy dishes, such as chilli con carne or a burrito, because the sweetness of the corn balances out the spice. It also makes a lovely side salad for a harvest-table spread.

---

2 COBS SWEET CORN

COCONUT OIL

100 GRAMS ROSA TOMATOES, QUARTERED

½ RED ONION, FINELY CHOPPED

1 HANDFUL FRESH CORIANDER LEAVES, CHOPPED

½ RED CHILLI, CHOPPED (OPTIONAL)

¼ CUP OLIVE OIL

1 TABLESPOON BALSAMIC VINEGAR

JUICE OF 1 LIME

Add the corn to a griddle pan over medium to high heat and lightly brush with coconut oil. Rotate the corn for about 10 minutes until the corn is charred. Once the corn is ready, set it aside to cool.

Add the tomatoes, onion, coriander, chilli, olive oil and balsamic to a medium-sized bowl and give it a good stir.

Remove the corn kernels by cutting them off the cob. Add the corn kernels and lime juice to the salsa and toss.

HEALTH FACT

After years of fad diets and carbs being vilified, I've learnt that the real villains are processed and refined carbohydrates, not the natural ones found in real food. At the end of the day, it is about balance and moderation. Rather than having guilt over eating a natural food such as sweet corn, try and cut out the unhealthy additions you pair it with.

HELLO HUMMUS

HUMMUS FIVE WAYS (VEGAN)

EACH VERSION SERVES 4

Hummus is a wonderful staple to have in your fridge. You can add it to salads and bowls, have it on a health cracker or simply dip some raw vegetables into it for lunch or a snack. You will never find my fridge without hummus in it.

TRADITIONAL (BASE) HUMMUS

250 GRAMS CHICKPEAS, COOKED

1 TABLESPOON TAHINI

6 TABLESPOONS OLIVE OIL

1 CLOVE GARLIC, PEELED

JUICE OF 1 LEMON

SALT AND PEPPER

Blend all the ingredients together in a food processor and season to taste.

Now that you have the base, it's time to get creative. Take the base hummus and add the extras to give it a gourmet touch, or simply enjoy on its own.

BEETROOT HUMMUS

2 LARGE BEETROOTS

1 QUANTITY TRADITIONAL (BASE) HUMMUS
   (SEE ABOVE)

1 TEASPOON GROUND CUMIN

Wrap the beetroots in foil and roast at 180 °C for 40 minutes or until soft. Once done, top and tail them and chop roughly, then blend with the base hummus and cumin.

ROASTED CARROT HUMMUS

3 LARGE CARROTS

4 CARDAMOM PODS

1 TABLESPOON COCONUT OIL

1 QUANTITY TRADITIONAL (BASE) HUMMUS
   (SEE ABOVE)

SALT AND PEPPER

OLIVE OIL

Toss the carrots and cardamom pods with the coconut oil and roast at 180 °C for 20–30 minutes. Cut off and discard the tops of the carrots. Blend the carrots with the base hummus and cardamom pods. Add salt and pepper to taste and drizzle olive oil on top.

PEA AND MINT HUMMUS

1 CUP PEAS, BLANCHED

¼ CUP FRESH MINT LEAVES

ZEST OF ½ LEMON

1 QUANTITY TRADITIONAL (BASE) HUMMUS
   (SEE ABOVE)

SALT AND PEPPER

Blend the peas, mint and lemon zest together with the base hummus. Add salt and pepper to taste.

SUN-DRIED TOMATO HUMMUS

1 QUANTITY TRADITIONAL (BASE) HUMMUS
   (SEE ABOVE)

50 GRAMS SUN-DRIED TOMATOES IN OIL

1 HANDFUL FRESH BASIL LEAVES

BALSAMIC VINEGAR

CAYENNE PEPPER

Blend the base hummus, tomatoes, basil and a splash of balsamic vinegar. Add cayenne pepper to taste.

BABA GANOUSH

AUBERGINE DIP (VEGAN)

SERVES 4

This is a traditional Middle Eastern dish made from aubergines, tahini and spices. It's a wonderful dip that you can serve with corn chips, pita bread or take with to a picnic. I love making my baba ganoush over a gas top, to impart the smoky flavour into the dish, but you can use a conventional oven with the grill function.

---

1 LARGE AUBERGINE

1 TABLESPOON TAHINI

1 CLOVE GARLIC, PEELED

1 HANDFUL FRESH FLAT-LEAF PARSLEY
   LEAVES, ROUGHLY CHOPPED

JUICE OF 1 LEMON

5 TABLESPOONS OLIVE OIL

SALT AND PEPPER

Preheat the oven to 190 °C.

Using tongs, char the aubergine on a gas stove directly over a medium flame, turning every 30 seconds, until the skin pulls back from the flesh. This will give the aubergine its traditional smoky flavour. Alternatively, the aubergine can be grilled in a regular oven after baking.

Once charred, place the aubergine onto a roasting tray and pop into the oven for 20–30 minutes or until soft.

Remove from the oven and place the aubergine into a plastic bag. Seal for 5–10 minutes, allowing it to steam. Once steamed, use a fork to remove the charred skin and discard. Add the aubergine flesh, tahini, garlic, parsley, lemon juice and olive oil to a blender and blend until smooth. Season to taste.

HEALTH FACT

Aubergines have a little bit of everything. They contain vitamins C, K and B6, and phosphorous, magnesium and thiamin. They are high in folic acid and iron. So if there ever was an all-rounder, this would be it.

PRESTO PESTO

PESTO THREE WAYS

SERVES 4

I've shared with you here pesto done three different ways. One is a traditional pesto, another is a slightly spicier tomato pesto, and the third is a nut-free option to accommodate nut allergies. You can also fold one of these pesto combinations through some freshly made pasta for a simple, flavoursome dish.

TRADITIONAL BASIL PESTO

2 CUPS FRESH BASIL LEAVES
½ CUP OLIVE OIL
½ CUP GRATED PARMESAN CHEESE
2 CLOVES GARLIC
½ CUP PINE NUTS, TOASTED
JUICE OF ¼ LEMON
SALT AND PEPPER

Add all the ingredients to a food processor and blend until smooth.

SUN-DRIED TOMATO PESTO

1 CUP SUN-DRIED TOMATOES IN OIL
⅓ CUP PINE NUTS, TOASTED
2 CLOVES GARLIC
¼ CUP OLIVE OIL
⅓ CUP GRATED PARMESAN CHEESE
1 TEASPOON CAYENNE PEPPER
SALT AND PEPPER

Add all the ingredients to a food processor and blend until smooth.

KALE AND SUNFLOWER SEED PESTO

1 CUP FRESH KALE LEAVES
⅓ CUP SUNFLOWER SEEDS
⅓ CUP GRATED PARMESAN CHEESE
2 CLOVES GARLIC
½ CUP OLIVE OIL
JUICE OF ½ LEMON
1 TEASPOON BALSAMIC VINEGAR
SALT AND PEPPER

Add all the ingredients to a food processor and blend until smooth.

HEALTH FACT

Basil benefits the stress hormone cortisol
and helps to reduce anxiety. Cortisol can be
good for short-term workouts, but when high
levels are present it can prevent fat burning
and cause irregular blood sugar levels.

SWEET AND SPICY KIKS

SWEET POTATO WEDGES WITH MANGO ATCHAR AND CASHEW NUTS (VEGAN)

SERVES 6–8

These sweet potatoes are one of my favourite things to make. You can top them with the dressing below or, if you don't want something spicy, simply drizzle over some olive oil and lemon zest or a few drops of truffle oil and Parmesan. Add a bit of freshness, such as coriander or baby spinach, and you'll have a gorgeous dish, ready to serve.

1 KILOGRAM SWEET POTATOES, WASHED
   AND CUT INTO WEDGES
2 TABLESPOONS COCONUT OIL
SALT AND PEPPER
50 GRAMS MANGO ATCHAR
¾ CUP COCONUT MILK
1 GENEROUS HANDFUL FRESH CORIANDER
   LEAVES
100 GRAMS RAW CASHEW NUTS, TOASTED
OLIVE OIL

Preheat the oven to 180 °C.

Place the sweet potatoes and coconut oil onto a roasting tray. Toss until the sweet potato is evenly covered and then season to taste. Pop the tray into the oven and roast for 45 minutes, turning them at the halfway mark.

While the sweet potatoes are roasting, add the mango atchar, coconut milk and half the coriander to a food processor. Blend until smooth and then season to taste.

Once the sweet potatoes are ready, add the wedges to a large salad bowl. Drizzle generously with the mango atchar sauce. You can use all of it or save some for later. It also depends on how hot you like it.

Roughly chop the remaining coriander and the cashews. Add them to the salad along with a good drizzle of olive oil. Season to taste and you are ready to feast!

HEALTH TIP

Cashew nuts are good for curbing sweet cravings because your body reads nuts as sweet foods. They're also high in energy and good fats.

OH, SWEET MUSTARD

HONEY MUSTARD CARROT BOWL (VEGAN)

SERVES 4

This honey mustard carrot bowl proves that you can make a dish delicious with minimal effort. All you really need to do is roast the vegetables in a simple dressing to bring out their flavours. This bowl is also very wholesome and packed with healthy ingredients. It has freshness, sweetness and crunch so enjoy it as a side or as the main event.

---

1 CUP BROWN LENTILS, RINSED
3 CUPS VEGETABLE STOCK
SALT AND PEPPER
400 GRAMS RAINBOW CARROTS, WASHED
1 MEDIUM-SIZED HEAD CAULIFLOWER
2 GENEROUS HANDFULS SWISS CHARD,
    ROUGHLY CHOPPED
80 GRAMS RAW ALMONDS, ROUGHLY
    CHOPPED

ROASTING DRESSING

1 TABLESPOON COCONUT OIL
2 TABLESPOONS HONEY
2 TABLESPOONS WHOLEGRAIN MUSTARD
SALT AND PEPPER

VINAIGRETTE

JUICE OF 1 LEMON
3 TABLESPOONS OLIVE OIL
SALT AND PEPPER

In a medium-sized saucepan over medium heat, add the lentils and vegetable stock. Simmer for 30 minutes. If the lentils dry out, add a little more hot water. Once ready, season to taste and set aside.

Preheat the oven to 180 °C.

Ready your vegetables. Top and tail the carrots and then cut into halves. Break the cauliflower into florets. Don't make the florets too small – bite-sized will do.

In a small bowl, mix together all the ingredients for the roasting dressing.

Add the cauliflower and carrots to a roasting tray and cover with the roasting dressing. Evenly coat the vegetables and pop them into the oven for 40 minutes, tossing at the halfway point. You want the ends to become sticky and crunchy.

Once ready, remove the vegetables from the oven and add the lentils to the roasting tray. Mix well.

Add the lentil mixture and the Swiss chard to a large bowl. Mix all the vinaigrette ingredients together, pour over the vegetables and give one final toss. Top with the chopped almonds to serve.

FOOD TIP

This is a prime example of how a cooked grain with a fresh green and roasted vegetables can make the most delicious meal. Vegetables and grains don't just have to be the side dishes, they can be the main event. Change your mindset from thinking every meal needs a vegetable, a starch and a meat and invite creativity into your bowl or onto your plate.

DRINKS

This chapter is short, but it's an important one. I hope that it does its job to show you that there are drink options for everyone in this chapter. There are hot teas and lattes, sparkling drinks and juices.

Often in our day-to-day lives we consume liquids without giving them much thought. These are healthy alternatives to your conventional juices or sodas that are often laden with preservatives, chemicals and sugars. More often than not we feel like we're choosing a healthier option by opting for diet sodas, but these pseudo-sugars can have an equally harmful effect on the body and are best avoided. Try to create drinks that are more about the flavour rather than simply trying to make something taste good by making it sweet. You'll find that you need a lot less sugar than you might think.

MANGO CHIA AND MINT JUICE

This is a seasonal drink, but you can also make it with other fruit and then add the chia seeds to the fruit juice.
The chia seeds will absorb the liquid and expand to keep you hydrated for longer.

2 RIPE MANGOS
4 CUPS WATER
3 SPRIGS FRESH MINT
¼ CUP CHIA SEEDS

Peel and blend the mangos. Add the mango purée, water, mint leaves and chia seeds to a large jug.

Let the mixture stand for 20 minutes to allow the chia seeds to absorb the liquid. If it is a little too thick for your liking, you can add more water.

Serve cold.

HEALTH TIP

Mango has excellent cancer-fighting properties and a high soluble-fibre content so is good for cholesterol. It is also very good for muscle cramps.

SPARKLING LIME AND POMEGRANATE

SERVES 6–8

This is a fun drink to illustrate how you can combine just a dash of real fruit juice with sparkling water to create a refreshing alternative to fizzy drinks, and it is a fun substitute to alcoholic drinks as well.

1 POMEGRANATE, SEEDED
¾ CUP FRESH POMEGRANATE JUICE
4 CUPS COLD SPARKLING WATER
1 LIME, SLICED

Add the pomegranate seeds, juice, sparkling water and lime slices to a large jug. Serve cold. You can add some ice cubes if you like.

HEALTH FACT

Sparkling water is a substitute for soda water. It cuts down the sugar or sugar-free additives that you would normally consume with soda and diet soda. The additives in sugar-free sodas trick your body into believing it's receiving sugar. Your body then prepares to digest the sugar that isn't there, releasing insulin into the bloodstream. Rather swap out the diet sodas for delicious and healthy alternatives. Also see the Infused Waters recipes (see page 163) for more tips and combinations.

GOLD AND GREEN LATTES

TURMERIC AND GINGER SERVES 1 | MATCHA SERVES 2

This turmeric and ginger latte is a great alternative if you are cutting out caffeine but still want a warm, comforting drink. It is creamy and spicy and has an element of decadence to it. You can easily double up the recipe. A matcha latte is a wonderful alternative to coffee, but note that it is not a caffeine-free option. If it makes you feel a bit jittery, rather opt for the turmeric and ginger latte.

TURMERIC AND GINGER LATTE

- 1½ CUPS ALMOND MILK
- 1 TEASPOON HONEY
- 1 TEASPOON FRESH OR GROUND TURMERIC
- 5 MILLIMETRE PIECE FRESH GINGER, SLICED
- 1 TEASPOON GROUND CINNAMON
- 1 TEASPOON VANILLA PASTE

In a medium-sized saucepan over medium heat, warm the almond milk. Do not let it boil. Add the honey, turmeric, ginger, cinnamon and vanilla paste to the milk and let it simmer gently for 5 minutes. Strain the mixture and discard the ginger. Once it is in the serving cup, use a frother to create foam. Serve hot.

MATCHA LATTE

- 1 CUP ALMOND MILK
- 1 CUP BOILING WATER
- 2 TEASPOONS MATCHA POWDER (BEST QUALITY YOU CAN FIND)
- 1 TABLESPOON HEMP SEEDS
- 10 RAW CASHEW NUTS
- 2 TEASPOONS AGAVE SYRUP OR HONEY
- 2 TEASPOONS COCONUT OIL
- 1 TEASPOON VANILLA PASTE

Warm the almond milk in a small saucepan over medium heat. Once hot, add all the remaining ingredients to a blender and blend until light and frothy. Serve hot.

HEALTH TIP

Turmeric is a natural anti-inflammatory and ginger neutralises gastrointestinal hormones, toxins and acids. Combining the two in this hearty, warm drink is not only very comforting, but also healthy and uplifting.

HEALTH TIP

Matcha has a high concentration of antioxidants and is a great replacement for caffeinated drinks. It can boost your metabolism and burn calories, and is a great detoxifier. Matcha calms the mind and relaxes the body.

PEPPERMINT TEA

SERVES 4

Peppermint tea has become a staple in my everyday life and is a wonderful drink to have without any added sugar or dairy.
I like to have it after dinner to help aid digestion, so give it a try if you're experiencing discomfort after a big meal. You can buy mint tea at
your local health store, but some of these have caffeine in them so if you want the caffeine-free version, fresh and real mint is the way to go.

2 SPRIGS FRESH PEPPERMINT
4 CUPS WATER

Boil the water and bruise the mint leaves to release their flavour. Add them to a tea pot or a tea cup along with the boiled water and enjoy!

HEALTH TIP

Peppermint tea is great for soothing digestive issues. It is refreshing and revitalising but also has a calming effect on the body. If you suffer from stomach cramps, an effective and soothing solution is to drink a fresh brew of peppermint tea.

HOMEMADE CHAI TEA

SERVES 5

This is the ultimate comfort drink for me. If I want a little pick-me-up or a sweetish drink then this is what I go for. It's relatively easy and extremely rewarding.

- 2 CENTIMETRE PIECE FRESH GINGER, SLICED
- 2 CINNAMON STICKS
- 2 TEASPOONS BLACK PEPPERCORNS
- 10 WHOLE CLOVES
- 6 CARDAMOM PODS
- 5 CUPS WATER
- 5 BLACK TEA BAGS
- 2 CUPS ALMOND MILK (OR FULL-CREAM MILK)
- HONEY

Add the ginger, cinnamon, black pepper, cloves and cardamom to a medium-sized saucepan along with the water. Bring to a simmer and let simmer for 5 minutes. Remove from the heat and add the tea bags. Steep for 10 minutes. Strain the liquid, discarding the solids, and add the milk and heat. Serve hot and add honey to taste.

HEALTH FACT

Chai tea has a very warm combination that helps curb sugar cravings. The spices give the body a sweet impression and tickles the taste buds.

INFUSED
WATERS

SERVES AS MANY AS YOU WOULD LIKE

Hydration is key for a healthy body. It can alleviate constipation and aid digestion. It also helps our skin glow and rids the body of toxins. Creating infused waters can not only make water colourful and beautiful to look at, but can also be a creative outlet. Play around with different combinations and see what your favourite is. You can add sparkling water to the mix, but remember that nothing is as good for you as regular H_2O so use it as often as possible as the base for your infusions.

I have used several ingredients in different combinations and amounts. Play around with them and with fruits that are in season. The longer you leave them to infuse the better they taste. If you use fresh ingredients, the flavours are even stronger and most of the time all you need to do is top up on the water before the fruit goes off.

HERE ARE A FEW OF THE COMBINATIONS I'VE USED:

GRAPEFRUIT AND ROSEMARY
LEMON, CUCUMBER AND MINT
FRESH GRANADILLA PULP WITH MINT
POMEGRANATE AND STRAWBERRY

You can add any fruit and spice you like, from oranges and limes to cinnamon and apple and even pineapple and rosemary! Just chop them up to release all the flavours and add them to your water jugs. Let them stand in the fridge for a few hours or even overnight to get the most flavour.

BERRIES

These little jewels are packed with antioxidants that help your body fight free radicals caused by stress.

CUCUMBER

This amazing fruit (yes, I said fruit) is filled with multiple B vitamins, such as B1, B5 and B7. It can help to reduce anxiety and stress and is very good for digestion.

GINGER

This marvellous ingredient has several health properties. It is a wonder in treating nausea and morning sickness, it can lower your risk of heart disease, aid exercise-induced muscle pain and menstrual pain, and it can even aid digestion. Just to name a few!

GRAPEFRUIT

Grapefruit acts as a tonic for the whole body. It lowers cholesterol and helps with the elimination of old blood cells. It is also packed with vitamin C.

LEMON

High in vitamin C, this citrus fruit is good for combating colds, rejuvenating skin cells and can even aid weight loss. Fresh lemon water in the morning will aid gut health.

LEMONGRASS

Don't be fooled by its hard exterior. Once cut, its flavours will be released. Lemongrass is wonderful for stomach ache, high blood pressure and can aid rheumatism.

MINT

Can relieve indigestion or an upset stomach and its wonderful flavour can be combined with most other fresh ingredients.

POMEGRANATE

This is an antioxidant-rich fruit. The seeds are sweet and wonderful to add to anything. You can also add them to your ice tray and make pomegranate ice. It looks beautiful and is so healthy for you.

TREAT BOWLS

Rather than calling empty foods 'treats', shift your perspective on what a treat is. Think about what a real treat is for your body – is it something that feeds it with nourishment or something that makes it sick with synthetic and high-sugar ingredients? I have learnt that there is always a healthier alternative to the sugary sweet treats that I crave. For all the baking staples, there is always a healthy alternative. Instead of cow's milk, use almond or coconut milk. Instead of refined sugar, try maple syrup or coconut sugar. And instead of bleached white flour, why not play around with spelt or almond flour?

Opting for the healthier choice doesn't leave me feeling unwell and my body thanks me for it. And, rest assured, you don't have to forego all the decadence that you want from a dessert.

STICKY MUD BOWL

VEGAN SWEET POTATO AND CHILLI BROWNIE BOWL (VEGAN)

SERVES 6-8

Who doesn't love a bowl of chocolate? This is the ultimate mud cake and is decadent and delicious. You can play around with the amount of maple syrup or sugar substitute you use if you want something less or more sweet, and the chilli adds another dimension to this chocolate-filled bowl.

500 GRAMS SWEET POTATO, PEELED

12 MEDJOOL DATES, PITTED

1 SMALL COURGETTE, GRATED

6 TABLESPOONS PURE MAPLE SYRUP

100 GRAMS ALMOND FLOUR (OR FLOUR SUBSTITUTE OF CHOICE)

2 TABLESPOONS COCONUT OIL

PINCH OF SALT

100 GRAMS GROUND OATS

6 TABLESPOONS RAW CACAO POWDER

½ TEASPOON CAYENNE PEPPER

40 GRAMS WALNUTS, CHOPPED

ICING

100 GRAMS QUALITY DARK CHOCOLATE, BROKEN INTO PIECES (I USE 70% DARK CHOCOLATE)

½ RED CHILLI, FINELY CHOPPED

Steam the sweet potato in a steamer for about 20 minutes until soft. When ready, allow to cool.

Preheat the oven to 180 °C. Line a 20 cm round baking tin with baking paper.

In a blender, add the dates and sweet potato and blend until smooth. If it gets a little sticky, add a dash of water to help it along.

In a bowl, mix together the courgette, maple syrup, flour, coconut oil, salt, oats, cacao powder, cayenne pepper and walnuts. Add the sweet potato mixture and mix everything together. You can use an electric beater, but a wooden spoon will work just as well.

Add the mixture to the baking tin and spread it evenly. Pop it into the oven for 45 minutes. When ready, let it cool for 10 minutes in the tin before removing and allowing it to cool completely on a cooling rack.

Meanwhile, melt the chocolate in a double boiler and add the chilli. Pour the chocolate over the mud cake and spread evenly. Allow to set, then cut into 4 cm squares to share.

HEALTH TIP

Almond flour is a great gluten-free replacement for regular wheat flour. If you find that gluten doesn't sit well with you, then give almond flour a try.

DATE NIGHT

SALTED CARAMEL TRUFFLE POPCORN BOWL (VEGETARIAN)

SERVES 2

This popcorn bowl is your secret weapon for any date night or movie night with your friends. You can keep the truffles separate or, as I like to do it, mix it all together in one bowl for a beautiful mix of treats.

1½ CUPS MEDJOOL DATES, PITTED
SALT
2 TABLESPOONS PEANUT BUTTER
    (UNSWEETENED)
100 GRAMS DARK CHOCOLATE, BROKEN
    INTO PIECES
COARSE SEA SALT
1 TABLESPOON COCONUT OIL
¼ CUP POPCORN KERNELS

Blend the dates in a food processor, adding a little boiling water if needed (1 teaspoon at a time) until you reach a thick, creamy consistency. Salt the dates to balance the sweetness – this creates the salted caramel (yes, this is vegan and it's amazing).

Use a teaspoon to make bite-sized truffle balls of date caramel and place onto wax paper.

In a small saucepan, heat the peanut butter to a runny consistency and drizzle the peanut butter over the truffles. Make sure you coat them all!

Place the chocolate in a bowl over a saucepan of simmering water. Let the chocolate sit for 5 minutes and then remove from the heat. Stir the chocolate until it is all melted and smooth.

Drizzle the chocolate over the truffles until they are completely covered and crack sea salt over them before they set. If they are not setting it can be because of a warm kitchen, so pop them into the fridge to help them along.

Mix the coconut oil and popcorn kernels in a saucepan on high heat. Once about half are popped, lift the saucepan while holding the lid down and swirl it to help the remaining kernels to settle to the bottom. Return to heat. When you no longer hear popping, give the pan a last swirl and take it off the heat.

Add the popcorn to a large bowl, followed by the truffles and press play.

HEALTH TIP

This is a snack you don't have to feel guilty about. All the ingredients have good properties so you can keep munching all the way to season six. Popcorn is high in protein and fibre and is significantly healthier for you than potato crisps. Make your own popcorn rather than buying microwavable popcorn, as those are filled with preservatives and unhealthy fats.

SAFFRON POACH

SAFFRON POACHED PEARS WITH WHIPPED COCONUT CREAM (VEGAN)

SERVES 2

This poached pear dessert is a decadent, elegant dessert that can be displayed beautifully. You can switch out the pears for apples if you wish, then serve them with the coconut ice cream from the Coconut Crumble recipe (see page 174) or simply whip up some cold coconut cream to accompany.

¾ CUP COCONUT CREAM

2 WHOLE PEARS, PEELED

5 CUPS WATER

½ CUP COCONUT SUGAR

3 WHOLE CLOVES

2 STAR ANISE

2 CINNAMON STICKS

4 CARDAMOM PODS

1 GENEROUS PINCH SAFFRON THREADS

Place the coconut cream in the freezer to chill. You do not want it frozen but you want the cream very cold or it will not whip.

In a medium-sized saucepan over medium heat, add the pears, water, coconut sugar, cloves, star anise, cinnamon, cardamom and saffron. Bring to a simmer for 35–40 minutes.

Once the pears are ready, remove them from the saucepan. Let the liquid simmer for another 5 minutes until it reaches a syrup-like consistency.

Meanwhile, remove the coconut cream from the freezer. Whisk the cream using a hand-held beater until soft peaks begin to form.

Serve the pears in a bowl topped with the whipped cream and drizzled with the saffron syrup.

HEALTH TIP

Cardamom is used as a natural breath freshener and prevents cavities while maintaining gum health. It is also good for a range of digestive issues and improves blood circulation.

THE TYLIE TART

VEGAN CHOCOLATE TART (VEGAN)

SERVES 6

This is a great example of how dark chocolate can upstage milk chocolate in any dessert. When you are shopping for your next chocolate treat, try and go for 70% dark chocolate or higher. I used 80% for this chocolate tart. You can pop this in the fridge to save it for later, if there's any left over.

CRUST

- 1 CUP RAW ALMONDS
- 7 MEDJOOL DATES, PITTED
- 3 TABLESPOONS DESICCATED COCONUT
- 2 TABLESPOONS COCONUT OIL, MELTED

FILLING

- 175 GRAMS DARK CHOCOLATE, BROKEN INTO PIECES
- 1 CUP COCONUT MILK
- 3 TABLESPOONS AGAVE SYRUP
- BERRIES TO DECORATE OR CRUSHED SEA SALT

Preheat the oven to 180 °C. Grease a 24 cm quiche tin.

To make the crust, place the almonds, dates and coconut in a food processor and blend until it forms fine crumbs. Add the coconut oil and blend until the mixture is sticky. You may need to use a spatula to make sure it has all mixed through.

Spoon the mixture into the quiche tin and flatten it with your fingers, packing it down evenly. Bake in the oven for 8 minutes. Once ready, set aside to cool.

For the filling, mix the chocolate and coconut milk in a heatproof bowl over a simmering saucepan of water. As soon as the chocolate is halfway melted, remove it from the heat and allow the residual heat to melt the rest of the chocolate. Add the agave and mix until all is combined.

Pour the filling into the crust. Gently tap the dish on the counter to knock out all the bubbles.

Refrigerate for at least 6 hours. Just before you serve the tart, decorate with the berries. If you have chosen to leave them off, you can also crack some salt over the tart.

HEALTH TIP

If you love chocolate, try to replace sugary milk chocolate with healthier dark chocolate. Not only will your palate adjust over time, but you will reap the benefits that cocoa has to offer and feel better in body and mind.

COCONUT CRUMBLE

APPLE AND PEAR COCONUT CRUMBLE WITH COCONUT ICE CREAM (VEGAN)

SERVES 10

This is my unique take on an apple crumble. I prefer using muscovado sugar as it caramelises the fruit beautifully, but coconut sugar will work as a substitute if you prefer a healthier option.

FILLING

- 6 MEDIUM TO LARGE APPLES
- 2 LARGE PEARS
- JUICE OF 1 LEMON
- 140 GRAMS COCONUT SUGAR (OR BROWN SUGAR)
- 3 TABLESPOONS SPELT FLOUR (OR CORNSTARCH)
- ¼ CUP FRESH APPLE JUICE
- 1 TEASPOON GROUND CINNAMON
- 1 VANILLA POD, SCORED LENGTHWAYS AND SEEDS REMOVED
- 1 TEASPOON GRATED FRESH GINGER

CRUMBLE

- 1 CUP ALMOND FLOUR
- 1 CUP ROLLED OATS
- ¼ CUP RAW COCONUT FLAKES
- ½ CUP SPELT FLOUR (OR ALL-PURPOSE FLOUR)
- ½ CUP COCONUT SUGAR (OR MAPLE SYRUP)
- ½ CUP MUSCOVADO SUGAR
- ½ CUP RAW PECAN NUTS
- 1 TEASPOON GROUND CINNAMON
- ½ CUP COCONUT OIL, MELTED
- PINCH OF SALT

COCONUT ICE CREAM (OPTIONAL)

- 160 MILLILITRES COCONUT OIL
- 180 MILLILITRES AGAVE SYRUP (OR HONEY)
- 80 GRAMS COCONUT SUGAR
- 300 GRAMS DESICCATED COCONUT
- 800 MILLILITRES COCONUT MILK
- PINCH OF SALT
- 2 TEASPOONS VANILLA PASTE

If you want to make the coconut ice cream to accompany the apple and pear crumble then prep it the day before as it needs quite a bit of time in the freezer. Place all the ingredients in a blender and blend until smooth. Pour into a medium-sized saucepan over medium to high heat and bring to a boil for 2 minutes. Remove from the heat and set aside to cool.

Once cooled, pour the mixture into an ice-cream maker and follow the manufacturer's instructions. If you don't have an ice-cream maker, you can pour the mixture into a freezer proof container and freeze for at least 3 hours. Mix it every 40 minutes to break up any ice crystals that may form. Remove from the freezer 10 minutes before serving, allowing it to soften.

For the apple crumble, preheat the oven to 180 °C. Grease a large pie dish.

Peel the apples and pears, remove the cores, and slice into thin wedges.

In a large mixing bowl, add the apples, pears and the remaining filling ingredients and mix together well. Set aside.

In a food processor, add all the ingredients for the crumble and pulse until just combined. You don't want the mixture to be too fine.

Spoon the filling into the pie dish and level the top. Top with the crumble mix and cover evenly.

Bake in the oven for 50 minutes or until the pears and apples are soft when pierced with a fork. Let rest for 30 minutes before serving. Scoop out your ice cream and serve with the apple crumble and try not eat it all out of the tub!

FOOD TIP

You can also serve the apple and pear crumble with whipped coconut cream. Make sure the coconut cream is cold before you whip it. If you need to chill it in a hurry, pop it into the freezer for 30 minutes. Using an electric whisk, beat the chilled coconut cream in a bowl until it stiffens.

DEATH BY NICE CREAM

PEANUT BUTTER ICE CREAM WITH HOT CHOCOLATE SAUCE (VEGAN)

SERVES 2

It was very surprising to me to see how perfect an ice cream can be without using the classic ice cream ingredients. You wouldn't guess that this ice cream doesn't have any dairy or refined sugars in it because it is made with such minimal effort with a dreamy result.

ICE CREAM

4 FROZEN BANANAS, SLICED

1 TEASPOON AGAVE SYRUP

1 TEASPOON VANILLA PASTE

2 TABLESPOONS PEANUT BUTTER OR
OTHER NUT BUTTER

2 TABLESPOONS COCOA POWDER

1 TEASPOON GROUND CINNAMON

30 GRAMS RAW ALMONDS, CHOPPED

CHOCOLATE SAUCE

80 GRAMS DARK CHOCOLATE, BROKEN
INTO PIECES

¼ CUP COCONUT MILK

Place the sliced bananas in a food processor and pulse for 15 seconds at a time until the bananas begin to break up. Add the agave, vanilla, nut butter, cocoa powder and cinnamon and increase the speed of the food processor. Once it reaches a creamy consistency, remove from the processor and transfer to a freezer proof container. Fold through the almonds. Flatten the mixture using a spatula and pop it into the freezer for 1 hour.

Melt the chocolate in a double boiler. Add the coconut milk and fold through.

Serve the ice cream cold with the hot chocolate sauce drizzled on top.

HEALTH FACT

Bananas, through many fad diets, have been vilified as a bad fruit due to their high sugar content, but they also have a very high potassium and fibre content. If eaten in moderation, they can be good for you and beneficial for blood pressure.

PARADISE PLATTER

FRUIT SALAD WITH TAHINI DRIZZLE (VEGETARIAN OR VEGAN)

SERVES AS MANY AS YOU WANT TO FEED

This is a chance for you to get creative and embrace the seasonal fruit at your local market. Fruit is filled with antioxidants, vitamins and fibre and, if eaten in moderation, can form a wonderful, fresh dessert that is not only beautiful to look at, but makes you feel good too. Choose a variety of colours, not only for the presentation, but also because different colours in fruit and vegetables offer different vitamins and minerals. Wash all of your fruit and vegetables, and have a moment of appreciation for the raw beauty of your fruit.

TAHINI DRIZZLE

- ¼ CUP TAHINI
- 1½ TABLESPOONS HONEY (OR AGAVE SYRUP)
- JUICE OF ½ LEMON
- ¼ TEASPOON GROUND CINNAMON
- PINCH OF GROUND GINGER
- 5 TABLESPOONS WATER

Add all the ingredients for the tahini drizzle to a jar, close the lid tightly and shake it up until it is mixed. This makes about 1 cup of dressing.

Slice up your fruit any way you choose and arrange it to create a beautiful fruit platter. Then drizzle the dressing over the top.

HUMMINGBIRD

SPICE CAKE WITH CASHEW CREAM CHEESE FROSTING (VEGETARIAN)

SERVES 10

This cake is the perfect example of how you can replace sugars and standard baking ingredients with healthier options, and make a delicious frosting without using the conventional milk, butter and powdered sugar.

CAKE

- 1½ CUPS SPELT FLOUR (OR ALL-PURPOSE FLOUR)
- 1½ TEASPOONS BICARBONATE OF SODA
- 1 TEASPOON BAKING POWDER
- ½ TEASPOON SALT
- 1 TEASPOON GROUND CINNAMON
- 1 CUP COCONUT SUGAR (OR MUSCOVADO SUGAR)
- 1 CUP MASHED BANANAS
- ¼ CUP COCONUT OIL, MELTED
- 1 TABLESPOON VANILLA PASTE
- ¼ CUP PLUS 2 TABLESPOONS PINEAPPLE JUICE, AT ROOM TEMPERATURE
- 2 TABLESPOONS APPLE CIDER VINEGAR
- ½ CUP CHOPPED FRESH PINEAPPLE (STEWED OR CANNED)
- ⅓ CUP RAW PECAN NUTS

FROSTING

- ½ CUP RAW MACADAMIA NUTS
- ½ CUP RAW CASHEW NUTS
- ¼ CUP PLUS 2 TABLESPOONS COCONUT MILK
- ¼ CUP MAPLE SYRUP
- 2 TABLESPOONS COCONUT OIL
- 1 TEASPOON VANILLA PASTE
- JUICE OF ½ LEMON
- ½ TEASPOON SALT

Soak the nuts for the frosting in water overnight or for 4 hours minimum. Once you're ready to work with them, drain and rinse them.

Preheat the oven to 180 °C. Grease a 25 cm bowl or cake tin and line the base with baking paper.

Sift the flour into a large bowl. Whisk in the bicarbonate of soda, baking powder, salt, cinnamon and sugar.

In a separate medium-sized bowl, whisk together the bananas, coconut oil, vanilla paste and pineapple juice until combined. Add the wet ingredients to the dry ingredients and mix well. Whisk in the apple cider vinegar, chopped pineapple and pecans. You should see little bubbles form.

Transfer the batter to the baking tin. Bake for 40–45 minutes or until a toothpick comes out clean when inserted. Remove from the tin and cool on a wire rack.

While the cake is cooling, combine all the ingredients for the frosting in a blender and blend until smooth. Pop the frosting into the fridge for 20 minutes to let it set.

Once the cake has cooled completely, ice it and serve.

FOOD TIP

This is a wonderful cake to make ahead of time and keep in the fridge. I recommend keeping the icing in the fridge because the creamy texture holds better when it is cold. The icing can change to a slightly brown colour, so if you want that beautiful white frosting, ice just before serving.

PINK CRUMBLE

STRAWBERRY AND RHUBARB CRUMBLE WITH WHIPPED COCONUT CREAM (VEGETARIAN OR VEGAN)

SERVES 6

Having crunch in a meal is so satisfying. Coupling that with the natural sweetness and soft texture of fruit makes you feel like you're eating a decadent dessert that will definitely have everyone wanting more.

WHIPPED COCONUT CREAM
- 400 MILLILITRES COCONUT CREAM, CHILLED

FILLING
- 4 CUPS FRESH STRAWBERRIES, STEMS REMOVED, AND DICED
- 2 CUPS DICED FRESH RHUBARB
- 2 TABLESPOONS FRESH ORANGE JUICE
- 2 TABLESPOONS HONEY (OR MAPLE SYRUP)
- 2 TABLESPOONS SPELT FLOUR
- 1 VANILLA POD, SCORED LENGTHWAYS AND SEEDS REMOVED

CRUMBLE
- 1 CUP ROLLED OATS
- ½ CUP ALMOND FLOUR
- 3 TABLESPOONS COCONUT OIL
- ¼ CUP MAPLE SYRUP (OR HONEY)
- 1 TEASPOON GROUND CINNAMON
- 1 TEASPOON VANILLA PASTE
- PINCH OF SALT

Serve this crumble with whipped coconut cream to add a new dimension. Make sure the coconut cream is chilled in the fridge for at least 1 hour, or in the freezer for about 30 minutes, before you start working with it.

Preheat the oven to 180 °C.

In a large bowl, combine all the ingredients for the filling and mix well.

In a food processor, add all the ingredients for the crumble and pulse until just combined.

In ovenproof serving bowls, add the filling and make an even layer in each. Top with the crumble and cover evenly. Bake for 40 minutes or until golden brown. Let them cool for 15 minutes before serving.

Empty the coconut cream into a bowl and whip until it forms stiff peaks. Serve on top of the hot rhubarb crumble.

FOOD TIP

Baking fruit in its own natural sugars and creating a healthy crumble is a wonderful way to combine different flavours and textures.

IT'S A DATE

COCONUT AND PEANUT BUTTER DATE BALLS (VEGETARIAN OR VEGAN)

MAKES 20 BITE-SIZED BALLS

Date balls are a power snack to have in the fridge and are simply delicious. If you feel like a lighter dessert after dinner, this is the perfect bite-sized option to satisfy your sweet tooth. You can play around with adding different elements and flavours if you like, such as fresh mint or orange zest.

¾ CUP RAW ALMONDS

¾ CUP HAZELNUTS (OR OTHER NUT OF
   YOUR CHOICE)

2 TABLESPOONS ROLLED OATS

2 TABLESPOONS CHIA SEEDS

1 CUP FRESH MEDJOOL DATES
   (12–15 DATES)

2 TABLESPOONS COCONUT OIL

1 TABLESPOON HEMP PROTEIN POWDER

2 TABLESPOONS PEANUT BUTTER (OR
   OTHER NUT BUTTER)

1 TABLESPOON HONEY (OR MAPLE SYRUP)

1 TABLESPOON RAW CACAO POWDER

½ CUP DESICCATED COCONUT

Add the almonds, hazelnuts, oats and chia seeds to a food processor and blend until a flour forms. Add the dates, coconut oil, protein powder, nut butter, honey and cacao powder and blend until a crumbly paste forms.

Add the desiccated coconut to a separate small bowl. Using your hands, form the date mixture into bite-sized balls and roll them in the coconut. Put them in the fridge for 15 minutes to let them set before serving. Or you can put them in an airtight container and keep them for later.

HEALTH FACT

Dates are highly nutritious and are a sweet treat you can feel good about. Ripe dates contain vitamins A, B, C and D, as well as folic acid, betacarotene, calcium, magnesium, potassium, iron ... the list goes on and on. If you like a sweet treat after dinner, a date is the perfect substitute and is delicious all by itself – just remember, everything in moderation.

BERRY BERRY NICE CREAM

BERRY ICE CREAM (VEGETARIAN OR VEGAN)

SERVES 3

This is a very quick and easy dessert to make. It's a great recipe for kids because it is sweet but packed with nutrients and a much healthier alternative to sugary, dairy-filled ice creams. But don't be fooled, the kids won't be the only ones who love it; the adults will be fighting over a scoop too!

2 LARGE BANANAS, FROZEN AND PEELED

2½ CUPS FROZEN BERRIES (BLUEBERRIES, RASPBERRIES, STRAWBERRIES)

2 TEASPOONS HONEY (OR COCONUT SUGAR)

JUICE OF 1 LIME

⅔ CUP COCONUT MILK

Add all the ingredients to a blender and blend until well combined and smooth. Pour the mixture into an ice-cream maker and follow the manufacturer's instructions. If you don't have an ice-cream maker, you can pour the mixture into a freezer proof container and freeze for at least 3 hours. Mix it every 40 minutes to break up any ice crystals that may form. Remove from the freezer 10 minutes before serving, allowing it to soften.

FOOD TIP

Not only do frozen bananas make a great base for dairy-free ice cream, but they are also wonderful to add to smoothies.

SWEET ANCIENT AMARANTH

CHOCOLATE AND CHERRY AMARANTH CUPS (VEGAN)

SERVES 2

These cups will make you and your guests feel special when you're presented with your own little pudding pot. You can experiment with your own flavour combinations, such as coffee, cherry, orange zest, mint or berries.

---

180 GRAMS FRESH CHERRIES

120 GRAMS AMARANTH

2 CUPS ALMOND MILK

100 GRAMS DARK CHOCOLATE, BROKEN
   INTO PIECES

1 TABLESPOON MAPLE SYRUP

1 TEASPOON VANILLA PASTE

PINCH OF SALT

Remove and discard the pits from half the cherries and then chop finely. Set aside.

In a medium-sized saucepan over medium heat, add the amaranth and almond milk. Simmer for 30 minutes.

Add the chocolate and stir until melted. Add the maple syrup, vanilla paste, salt and chopped cherries and fold through. Turn off the heat and cover with a lid for another 5 minutes.

Once ready, serve in small ramekins and decorate with the remaining whole fresh cherries. If cherries are out of season, you can add orange zest instead or fold through a handful of fresh mint leaves.

HEALTH TIP

Amaranth is an ancient grain that is very high in magnesium. Paired with dark chocolate, it makes a great base for different flavour combinations to complement your chocolatey bowl.

INDEX

BIBLIOGRAPHY

Brazier, B. (2011) *Thrive Foods: 200 Plant-Based Recipes for Peak Health.* USA: Da Capo Press.
Craig, I., and Jesson, R. (2016) *Wholesome Nutrition For You.* Cape Town: Penguin Random House South Africa.
Hart, J. (2014) *Eat Pretty – Nutrition for Beauty, Inside and Out.* California: Chronicle Books LLC.
Roberts, M. (2012) *Healing Foods.* Pretoria: Briza Publications.
William, A. (2016) *Medical Medium – Life-Changing Foods.* USA: Hay House Incorporated.